Credit Analysis

WILEY PROFESSIONAL BANKING AND FINANCE SERIES
EDWARD I. ALTMAN, Editor

THE STOCK MARKET, 4TH EDITION
Richard J. Teweles and Edward S. Bradley

TAX SHELTERED FINANCING THROUGH THE R & D LIMITED PARTNERSHIP
James K. La Fleur

CORPORATE FINANCIAL DISTRESS: A COMPLETE GUIDE TO PREDICTING, AVOIDING, AND DEALING WITH BANKRUPTCY
Edward I. Altman

CREDIT ANALYSIS: A COMPLETE GUIDE
Roger H. Hale

Credit Analysis
A Complete Guide

ROGER H. HALE

A Wiley-Interscience Publication
JOHN WILEY & SONS
New York • Chichester • Brisbane • Toronto • Singapore

Library of Congress Cataloging in Publication Data:

Hale, Roger H.
Credit analysis.

(Wiley professional banking and finance series)
"A Wiley-Interscience publication."
Includes bibliographical references and index.
1. Bank loans—Handbooks, manuals, etc. 2. Credit—Handbooks, manuals, etc. 3. Credit bureaus—Handbooks, manuals, etc. I. Title. II. Series.
HG1641.H255 1983 658.8'8 83-10217
ISBN: 978-0-470-93740-2

20 19 18 17

Series Preface

The worlds of banking and finance have changed dramatically during the past few years, and no doubt this turbulence will continue through the 1980s. We have established the Wiley Professional Banking and Finance Series to aid in characterizing this dynamic environment and to further the understanding of the emerging structures, issues, and content for the professional financial community.

We envision three types of books in this series. First, we are commissioning distinguished experts in a broad range of fields to assemble a number of authorities to write specific primers on related topics. For example, some of the early handbook-type volumes in the series concentrate on the Stock Market, Investment Banking, and Financial Depository Institutions. A second type of book attempts to combine text material with appropriate empirical and case studies written by practitioners in relevant fields. An early example is a forthcoming volume on The Management of Cash and Other Short-Term Assets. Finally, we are encouraging definitive, authoritative works on specialized subjects for practitioners and theorists.

It is a distinct pleasure and honor for me to assist John Wiley & Sons, Inc. in this important endeavor. In addition to banking and financial practitioners, we think business students and faculty will benefit from this series. Most of all, though, we hope this series will become a primary source in the 1980s for the members of the professional financial community to refer to theories and data and to integrate important aspects of the central changes in our financial world.

EDWARD I. ALTMAN

Professor of Finance
New York University
Schools of Business

Preface

This is a book about credit: It is not about accounting or about law relating to banking. The reason is that there seems to be a genuine lack of published material on credit, and this book is intended to fill that gap. Because credit decisions are the reflection of personal judgment about a borrower's ability to repay, it ought to be possible to write in general terms about this subject without relating the material just to the business environment of one country. For, after all, business risks are of the same type although not of the same magnitude all over the world. The aim is, therefore, to assist bankers and credit analysts to make credit decisions by writing about a universal form of credit analysis. As a result of its approach to the study of risk, this book should also be valuable to long-term lenders and bond market investors, as well as to those who are undertaking a business school program with special emphasis on finance.

The idea for this book came one wet weekend in the Philippines, where I was working for two months to start up an Asian credit training program. It was clear that there was keen interest from foreign bankers to learn the U.S. bank credit analysis system so as to apply this within their own countries. However, most available material was not written for such an audience and was primarily oriented toward the U.S. domestic banking scene. Further, it was frequently full of jargon and not suitable for people for whom English is a second language. Accordingly, as I had had the privilege of teaching credit to trainees from more than 20 countries over the previous three years, and as I had learned the U.S. system after several years in a British bank, it seemed appropriate to attempt the task of writing a general guidebook that could be applied in any country. Furthermore, in order to make it a practical book, problems and case studies have been included to illustrate the points made.

All the views expressed in this book are my own rather than any expression of the policy of the major New York bank for which I work. However, I would like to thank many colleagues for their ideas and constructive criticism. I would also like to thank Stauffer Chemical Company and Northern Engineering Industries Limited for permission to use their financial statements as examples.

One word of warning: References will be made frequently to Generally Accepted Accounting Principles (GAAP) as issued by the U.S. Financial Accounting Standards Board. Readers should become familiar with U.S. accounting principles in order to get the best out of this book.

ROGER H. HALE

Oldwick, New Jersey
August 1983

1 What Is Credit Analysis?

If a pawnbroker lends money against a gold watch, he does not need credit analysis. He needs instead to know the value of the watch. But if a banker lends money either to a person or to a corporation, the banker needs credit analysis to help determine the risks involved with the loan and the likelihood of repayment.

If credit is, as the English philosopher John Locke wrote in the seventeenth century, "nothing but the expectation of a sum of money within some limited time,"[1] then credit analysis is the process of inquiry prior to making the decision to lend. In this inquiry, the banker today does his best to replace emotional feelings, such as hopes and fears, with reasoned arguments based upon a careful study of a borrower's strengths and weaknesses.

The fundamentals of modern credit analysis are twofold: First is the examination of the nature of the borrower's business in the context of its industry, and second is the analysis of cash flow. The purpose of the former is to understand the comparative market position of the firm, the pressures of competition, the risk and reward structure of the industry, the barriers to entry, the degree of technological change, and so on. The purpose of cashflow analysis, on the other hand, is to disentangle from financial statements based on historical accounting principles the actual movements of cash in terms of its sources and uses. Once these past sources and uses have been examined, a reasonable estimate can be made as to future sources and uses, and this can be combined with the understanding of the borrower already gained to permit a judgment to be made as to the borrower's credit worthiness.

It was not always so. In the old days, bankers relied extensively on secured lending, which, as I have suggested, requires only a good valuation of the security being offered rather than a knowledge of credit. Then, too, financial statements, standards of disclosure of information, and the amount of market information which is generally available have all changed radically in the past 50 years, especially in industrialized countries. As a result, a much

[1]Quoted in *A Dictionary of the English Language*, Samuel Johnson, London, 1773.

more detailed comparison is now possible based on financial ratio calculations, but at the same time, the reader must also be warned that financial analysis is only part of the process.

In the old days, too, money was traditionally available from banks for only short periods of up to a year and usually was related to seasonal borrowings. As a result, early textbooks on banking, besides spending many chapters describing the legal requirements of secured loans, usually concentrated on the seasonal borrower. In such cases, most attention was paid to the balance sheet and in particular to the working capital of the firm. To quote an example from a 1924 textbook, "It is necessary for the credit man to 'shade the assets,' or to write off a certain percentage merely as a precautionary measure. The important factor is not the applicant's opinion as to the value of his assets, which the listed valuation all too frequently represents, but the actual value that will ultimately be realised from them."

At that time, the main concern was working capital. Was there enough? How would it change if conditions changed? How much would be left if the assets were written down? The emphasis thus was placed upon the ability of a company to repay its debts if liquidation were to occur. As A. S. Dewing observed: "Bankers have proverbially been interested in statements of the net worth of a business at liquidation—as if the fundamental value of a working horse were its value for fertilizer."[2] Unfortunately, this tended to concentrate the analyst's mind on the balance sheet and not on the income statements. Therefore, the analyst was looking at a static situation, not a dynamic one. At best, three years of balance sheets would be compared, but too little emphasis would be placed on the income statements, which are the bridge connecting each static situation. And cashflow was not really discussed at all.

One limitation of this approach was that it was not possible to know whether working capital was adequate. Some financial analysts claimed that, if current assets were double the figure of current liabilities, thus giving a current ratio of two to one, this could be taken to mean that working capital was adequate. They argued that, in case of bankruptcy, falling prices, or inflated figures, the book value of current assets could shrink by 50% in liquidation, and current creditors, provided there were no long-term creditors, would still receive payment of their obligation in full.

Such an approach has several weaknesses. First, it pays no regard to the quality of the assets. Current assets such as short-term investments which are readily marketable without further cost or work being undertaken have quite a different quality from assets such as work in progress or partly finished goods for which no market may exist. Companies often fail because their products fail. In these circumstances, the value of their inventories will bear no relation to recorded values. If the products failed to sell when the firm

[2]*The Financial Policy of Corporations*, 5th ed., Vol. 2, A. S. Dewing, Copyright © 1953 Ronald Press. Reprinted by permission of John Wiley & Sons, Inc.

was a going concern, then how much more likely is it that they will fail to sell when the firm is, as they say, a "gone" concern.

Second, the approach pays no regard to the nature of the liabilities. Some liabilities are much more current than others. One person to whom the liability is owed may have very strong bargaining power. Another may have a pressing need for payment and cannot wait. While the government is often a creditor of a firm—for taxes due or social security payments—and has strong bargaining power, it seldom exercises this by putting firms into liquidation. However, a supplier of goods—especially one that is bigger than the firm, has been extending credit for large amounts, and is the sole supplier available—can have a great deal of power. One might say that such liabilities are the most current of all in that if they are not settled regularly, the supplies of goods will cease. But these situations are rare. It is nearly always the banks, not the suppliers, who put firms into liquidation. Indeed, as one witty and experienced banker once remarked, "The principal asset of many insolvent firms is the forbearance of their creditors."

CASHFLOW ANALYSIS

Working capital analysis and the current ratio, then, were the core of the old system. But they were often found to be insufficient. The depression of the 1930s, the rapid expansion of nearly all types of business in the 1945–1955 period, and increased international trade and competition brought about a searching reappraisal of all types of business practices. Many creditors found that they suffered losses even when they lent to businesses with "adequate" working capital. Demand for credit was changing also. Whereas short-term lending had been the order of the day in the 1930s and 1940s, with the emergence of the 1950s, demand for longer term funds from banks began to appear. This happened first in the United States, and then as American banks moved overseas, taking their term lending techniques with them, it was found that business firms in most other countries had needs for bank credit of longer than one year.

To quote A. S. Dewing again,

> The Banker has come to understand that the basis of credit is the presumption that earning power will continue, it is not based on the amount of working capital nor on the liquidity of any kind of capital as such. Ultimately he has come to recognise that such a loan can be paid except through other borrowings only over the comparatively long period during which the earnings can accumulate. Whatever may have been the tradition of banking, the basis of value upon which the credit of the corporation must ultimately rest, is the earning power.[3]

[3]*The Financial Policy of Corporations*, 5th ed., Vol. 1, A. S. Dewing, Copyright © 1953 Ronald Press. Reprinted by permission of John Wiley & Sons, Inc.

This was indeed an improvement upon the static balance sheet analysis. From this approach grew more reliance upon debt service coverage ratios and the total amount of long-term debt in relation to the overall long-term sources of funds available to the firm (that is, equity). Debt service coverage ratios compare a firm's available income with the demands of interest payments and capital requirements. Although they are useful ratios, they suffer from comparing two things which are not of like nature. Interest payments need to be made in cash, and income is based on accounting principles that are not related to cash movements. With the emergence of the 1950s, cashflow first became more important in the short-term analysis of bankers. It was given strong emphasis in the 1953 textbook *Introduction to Business Finance.*[4] The authors B. B. Howard and M. Upton made this statement:

> It should be clear that the real problem in judging a business's short term financial position is to ascertain as closely as possible the future cash generating ability of the business in relation to the claims upon that cash that will have to be met in the near future. . . . It matters not what conditions prevail at a given time; the important thing is whether the business in performing its regular operating functions can continue to generate cash in sufficient quantity and in satisfactory time to meet all operating and financial obligations.

It was another decade before long-term capital markets also reflected the cashflow approach. In a classic *Harvard Business Review* article of 1962,[5] Donaldson discussed the viewpoint of the corporate treasurer in looking at the debt capacity of the firm. Pointing out the inadequacies of traditional debt capacity decision rules for purposes of internal debt policy, Donaldson stated that the basic question to be answered in the appraisal of the magnitude of risk associated with long-term debt could be posed with deceptive simplicity: "What are the chances of the business running out of cash in the foreseeable future?" Donaldson highlighted the fact that debt service coverage ratios related to accounting income, not cash, and that debt had to be serviced with cash. His new approach based the maximum debt capacity on what management can estimate to be the "maximum adverse limits of recession behavior covering each factor affecting cashflow." In other words, this approach required management to make worst-case projections to see what cashflows would still be available for servicing long-term debt.

> Suppose a company has been assuming, as many do, that it can safely incur longterm debt up to a maximum of 30% of capitalization. This rule can be translated into its equivalent of dollars of annual debt servicing charges and directly compared with the results of the recession cashflow analysis. In view

[4]B. B. Howard and M. Upton. *Introduction to Business Finance.* New York: McGraw-Hill, 1953, p. 135. Reproduced with permission.

[5]Reprinted by permission of *Harvard Business Review.* Excerpt from "New Framework for Corporate Debt Policy" by Gordon Donaldson (March/April 1962), Copyright © 1962 by the President and Fellows of Harvard College. All rights reserved.

of the fact that the rule probably has been derived from external sources, it is likely that the annual debt servicing which it permits either exceeds or falls short of the amount of cashflow indicated by the internal analysis.

In view of the approximate nature of the analysis however, this is not likely [illegible] nge in debt policy unless the amount of the variation is sub-

[illegible] are now widely accepted as the proper basis for assessing [illegible] orporations. A balance sheet by itself does not provide this [illegible] ion because it says nothing about cash-generating ability. [illegible] which a company will receive over the next 12 months is [illegible] by balance sheet assets as of the date of that balance sheet, [illegible] he obligations to be paid are not shown as liabilities since [illegible] t that time come into existence. Such obligations are, for instance, the regular payments to suppliers and employees and the purchase of capital equipment.

In the same way, sales are the basic source of cashflow, and a balance sheet tells little about sales. The former notion that current assets are the source from which current liabilities are paid is not very useful. Current liabilities are not paid with current assets—they are paid with cash. It is the cash conversion cycle that demands the analyst's attention. This cycle is the process of buying goods, converting them, adding value, selling them, and collecting the proceeds of sale. In the course of this cycle, current assets are constantly being created and replaced. (This will be discussed further in Chapter 6.)

Cashflow from operations is the phrase chosen by analysts to cover the cash resulting from normal sales of goods in any period, less the cash paid out to settle operating liabilities in that period. As will be seen, this cashflow is not the same as profit, nor is it necessary or likely that the operating cash outflow in any one period is related to the same set of goods and services that caused cash to flow in. Cashflow from operations under normal conditions provides the banker's source of repayment. In this, we include seasonal loans, where short-term debt is repaid by the reduction in the level of current assets (inventory and accounts receivable) at the end of the season, as inventories are reduced and accounts receivable are collected. To find a company's cashflow from operations, it is necessary to have two balance sheets and an income statement for that period. How to use these is explained in Chapter 3.

Earlier, reference was made to the earning power of the corporation. Now we are saying that cashflow is more important than earnings. This deserves some explanation. There is not necessarily a contradiction here. In the long run, companies that do not have the ability to generate earnings will die,

[6]Reprinted by permission of *Harvard Business Review.* Excerpt from "New Framework for Corporate Debt Policy" by Gordon Donaldson (March/April 1962), Copyright © 1962 by the President and Fellows of Harvard College. All rights reserved.

either by dissolution or through being acquired by another company. In the long run, too, a dollar has been or is expected to be received at some time during the life of the enterprise for each dollar of revenue recognized by accounting principles during a given period, and a dollar either has been or will be paid out at some time for every dollar of expense matched with that revenue. However, because of the leads and lags between cash payments and the definition of a cash payment as an expense, the amount of cash generated by a company in a short period of time, such as a year, will equal accounting profit only by accident. And furthermore, while monetary profits for the actual lifetime of the firm must equal its net cashflows over the same period, profitable firms, as will be seen later, can have large cash outflows over extended periods of time as a result of the need to build up inventories for future growth. Indeed, some levels of sales growth are unsustainable without negative cashflows, even for very profitable firms. In the short-term, therefore, cashflows are more important than earnings. The principal reason is that earnings can be manipulated by management's choice of accounting policies, whereas cashflow cannot be changed by any accounting policy. Examples of these policies are discussed in the section on the nature of accounting principles in Chapter 2.

Identifying Risks

After recognizing the importance of cashflow in the analysis of credit, the next feature to study is the degree and type of risks affecting that cashflow. Bear in mind that, in statistics, risk is measured by the probability of certain outcomes. Probability itself represents the extent to which an outcome can be predicted on the basis of observations of historic results and their distribution around a mean or average figure. It is an accepted principle that the more certain a future cashflow is, the greater the funds that can be borrowed against it. Indeed, the basis for modern investment analysis involves the discounting of future cashflows so as to make capital budgeting decisions and recognizes that more risky future cashflows require higher rates of discount. It follows, therefore, that as analysts you should try to list and quantify the risks affecting the firms you are studying.

Business risks are very diverse. You need more than an organized approach to judge which risks are important in any situation. You also need good judgment. The following list simply presents one way of looking at business risks, but the suggested questions regarding risk are certainly not exhaustive. It is based on the four major functional disciplines of business—namely, production, marketing, personnel, and finance—plus the influence of government.

Production. Does the business have one or many sources for supplies of materials? What is the effect of changes in the cost of power and fuel? What is the main element in production costs? Capital? Labor? Is there rapid technological change? How costly is it to innovate? How dependent is the business on other firms? What are the effects of research and development? What is the effect of volume changes on the cost structure? What risks affect the location of the plant?

Marketing. What factors affect industry sales? Are sales highly variable? Is demand price elastic? Is income elastic? What are substitute products? Are imports significant? What are the competitors' strategies? What are the barriers to entry of new competitors? What changes in customer needs could happen? Are buyers more powerful than suppliers? What is a source of strength in this market? How vulnerable is it? What is the risk of losing a major customer?

Personnel. What causes labor turnover? What causes productivity increases? What is the motivation of employees? What is the risk of strikes? When will labor contracts expire? How dependent is the firm on certain key individuals?

Finance. How vulnerable is the firm to interest rates? How much access to outside capital does it have? How dependent is it on a single large project? How diversified are revenue sources? How vulnerable is it to customer credit losses?

Government Action. In what ways could the government or its agencies affect the firm? Monopoly or antitrust regulation? Economic policy? Protection from imports? Export subsidiaries? Government contracts? State-owned competitors? Tax on output? Excise duty? Licensing of new products? License to do business?

In thinking about such risks, you would do well to try and quantify the degree of probability of the events which affect cashflow.

Comparative Analysis

All businesses face risks. Every member of an industry faces risks, although obviously the successful members have overcome these risks better than the unsuccessful. To judge the credit worthiness of a company, you have to look at it in the context of its industry through the process of comparative analysis. This is similar to the way a doctor must compare a patient's medical test results against the results for a healthy person so as to judge the patient's current state of health. In credit analysis, it is normal to use financial ratios to compare companies within the same industry. Choosing and using financial ratios is discussed in Chapter 5. For the moment, however, it will be sufficient to introduce an alternative to simple financial ratios to illustrate how it is possible to compare members of the same industry by rating each of them on what analysts consider to be key strengths or key elements within that industry. For example, let's look at the worldwide heavy equipment industry. Table 1.1 shows the key elements chosen by experienced industry analysts.

Table 1.1 Variables in Industry Analysis

Marketing Variables	*Production Variables*
Product quality	Capacity
Product line comparison	Operating leverage
Price	Degree of integration
End sales financing	Automation
Dealer network	Sourcing
Advertising	Economies of scale
Market share	Labor relations
Financial Variables	*Strategic Variables*
Size of assets	Research
Profitability	Management
Debt capacity	Government support
Access to capital markets	Marketing strategy
Ownership	
Capital spending requirements	
Characteristics of banking group	
Foreign exchange effects	

After listing the features, the analysts assigned numerical ratings to each feature for each company according to its perceived strength, adjusting each rating for how accurate they thought their perception to be. Variables were also given different weightings according to their perceived importance. Companies then emerged with a credit score, and for portfolio analysis purposes, a bank is able to compare the extent of its exposure to each member of the industry against the perceived strength of that member.

Comparative analysis also includes comparing the latest financial results of a company with its own track record, using a form of "spread sheet" described in Chapter 2. This is sometimes called horizontal analysis, because the comparison with prior years' performance is made by looking horizontally across the columns for each year. By contrast, vertical analysis is the process of determining what caused changes in the current year's results. This is discussed further in the following chapters.

CREDIT ANALYSIS WITHIN THE LENDING FUNCTION

There was a time a few years back when competition between banks for lending to businesses was less severe than today. Bank marketing departments did not exist, and bankers did not go out to call on prospects. Companies were expected to prepare their own loan applications, and generally they chose to stay loyal to those banks which had been with them for some years. Indeed, if a company approached a bank with whom it had had no previous relationship, it was generally assumed that this must be a poor credit risk, since why else would it want to leave its existing bank?

In our increasingly competitive environment, however, all that has changed, and it is now the bankers who call on the customers rather than vice versa. The lending process has therefore developed into a four-stage affair: (1) the development of new business; (2) the process of credit evaluation, including an annual review of the borrower; (3) the pricing and structuring of the loan or line of credit; and (4) the obtaining of repayment. Regrettably, the fourth stage can deteriorate into work-out and even charge-off. *Work out* is the process whereby, because the borrower has failed significantly with its repayment plans, the lender is obliged to work out the problem by some kind of restructuring, renegotiation, or even ultimately liquidation of the company. *Charge-off* is the term used to designate amounts written off as uncollectible—that is, bad loans. Obviously, no bank wants bad loans, but in the nature of things, every bank has them. If it does not, it is likely that it is too risk averse and is possibly contracting in size. Credit analysis is intended to keep the number of bad loans to a minimum and to highlight a potential problem early enough to enable the lender to seek early repayment or withdrawal from the credit. Getting out of problem loans is the supreme test of the bank lending officer, and to this extent, every bank officer should maintain his or her credit skills.

From time to time, there is debate about whether a lending institution should be organized with two separate functions—namely, a business development group and a credit department. The business development group, consisting of account officers, is charged with the responsibility of marketing and selling financial services, including credit products, while the credit department performs analyses and decides which borrowers are acceptable. The alternative structure is one without a credit department but where each officer accepts responsibility for his or her lending decisions, including performing the credit analysis (or at least supervising and reviewing it).

Both structures have their weaknesses. The two-function approach tends to generate fierce conflict between those who want to develop new business (that is, sell loans) and those who want to keep risk acceptable. In prosperous times, the marketing people have the dominant organizational position, but in recessions, the credit department becomes more powerful. Besides this conflict, there are also other problems: The business development group usually does not consider itself responsible for asset quality, may well be judged for its performance on increasing loan volume, tends to have more organizational influence, especially in growth-oriented institutions, and feels superior to the credit department.

On the other hand, the delegated responsibility approach, where account officers accept the need for quality as well as volume in their loan portfolios, has the weakness that its success depends on having experienced account officers. Without them—the seasoned lenders—credit policy can become very weak, especially if the credit decision process is structured so that too much authority is delegated to junior officers. Some U.S. banks experienced severe problems in the early 1980s in part because the credit function was poorly structured within the organization. Having said that, however, I must add that there is no golden rule, other than that the corporate strategy of the lending institution should determine its credit decision-making structure.

2 Examining the Evidence

I keep six honest serving men,
(They taught me all I knew):
Their names are What and Why and When
And How and Where and Who.
RUDYARD KIPLING

In order to complete financial analysis successfully and thoroughly, you must begin by examining the evidence as if you were a detective. This does not, of course, mean believing that you are examining the scene of a crime, but you might say that it is dangerous to accept evidence at face value, and tests must be performed on what is found in order to establish its usefulness.

The principal evidence available to the analyst is always the company's financial statements or Annual Report and Accounts—and, therefore, it is to these that we turn first.

FINANCIAL STATEMENTS

It must be stated at once that there is absolutely no substitute for reading the company's Annual Report from cover to cover, including and indeed paying especially close attention to items in small print. A typical public company's Annual Report, of course, contains considerably more than financial statements, including generally such items as a Chairman's statement, a historical record of five or more years, pictures of happy employees or the company's gleaming products, charts, graphs, and various other information, much of which will be useful to the analyst in learning about nonfinancial aspects of the company.

On the other hand, privately controlled companies, which are not obliged to disclose information to the same extent as publicly owned companies, will be much more discreet and generally limit themselves to the minimum disclosure required by the laws of the country of residence. This semisecrecy is sometimes seen as common sense on the grounds that "what you don't tell can't hurt you," but often it is also considered wise for a company not to give competitors and critics any ammunition that they could use against the company.

Frequently, whether dealing with public or private companies, you will be looking for certain information and will find it is not disclosed in the financial statements available. Rightly, you will ask yourself "I wonder why not," and it is the answer to this question that will help you understand the company. There are several very successful firms that probably attribute part of their success to a policy of nondisclosure, among which the best-known are Michelin and Hallmark Cards, and thus in no way should the absence of information be considered by itself a credit weakness. You must be satisfied that the reason for disclosure or nondisclosure of information is a legitimate one, and to this end, you must always consider for whom the financial statements were produced. This is particularly true in countries where strict accounting standards are unknown; here, rumor has it, there are often three sets of books kept by the bookkeeper—one for the tax collector, one for the banker, and one for the actual owners of the business.

WHERE TO START

Given a public company's Annual Report, you might wonder where to start. A good place is often the Auditor's Opinion, followed by the page disclosing the company's principal accounting policies. Bearing in mind that no management would use anything except management accounting for making decisions in running the business, you should at once recognize that these figures are being produced by management for others to read and are based on financial accounting principles, not management accounting principles. It is appropriate, therefore, at the outset to see first whether management has been given a clean report by the outside auditors, one of whose jobs it is to check that the figures "present fairly" the results for the year, and then to determine whether the accounting principles employed seem reasonable for the kind of industry being examined.

Next, it is sensible to get a simple profile of the company by turning to the balance sheet to answer three questions: How large? How profitable? How solvent? Proper measures of size, profitability, and solvency are discussed in Chapter 5, but suffice it to say at this point that a rapidly growing, profitable but rather insolvent company may have good reasons to choose accounting principles that are different from those chosen by a large, steady but highly solvent company. The most obvious reason that comes to mind is that the former will be more conscious of presenting itself to investors in a highly attractive form because of its probable need for new equity capital. In other words, it will want to make its profits look as good as possible.

THE AUDITOR'S OPINION

It has already been stated that one of the auditor's tasks is to see that the financial statements present fairly the financial position. The auditor has other tasks as well, but contrary to popular belief, these do not normally

FINANCIAL REPORT

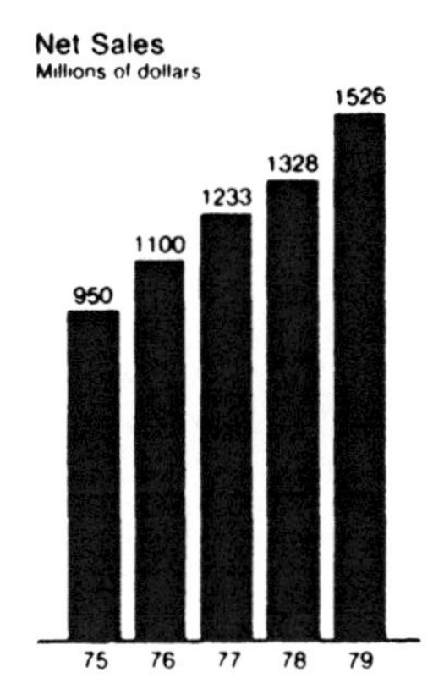

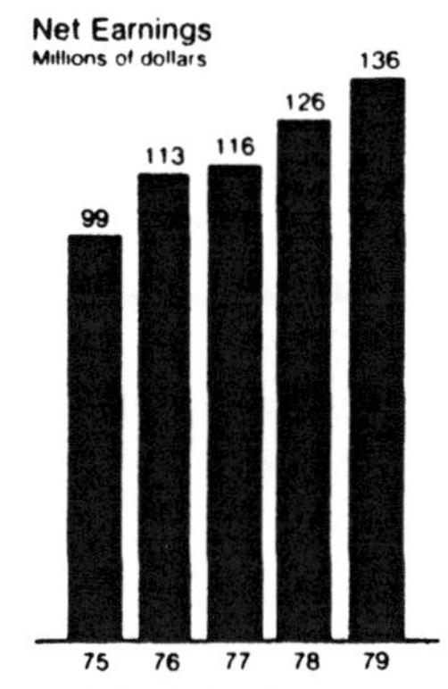

Statement of management responsibility for financial statements

The accompanying financial statements of Stauffer Chemical Company and subsidiaries for the years ended December 31, 1979 and 1978, were prepared by management in conformity with generally accepted accounting principles.

The Company is responsible for the integrity and objectivity of its financial statements. In preparing these financial statements, management makes informed judgments and estimates of the expected effects of events and transactions that are currently being accounted for.

The Company maintains systems of internal accounting controls which are designed to provide reasonable assurance that assets are safeguarded and records reflect in all material respects the transactions of the Company, in accordance with management's authorizations. These systems include formal policies and procedures, organizational structures that provide an appropriate division of responsibility, careful selection and training of qualified personnel, and an extensive program of internal audits and appropriate management follow-up. The Company believes its systems provide reasonable assurance that assets are safeguarded and that its records are reliable.

The Board of Directors, through its Operating and Audit Committees, monitors the financial and accounting administration of the Company, including the review of the activities of both the internal auditors and the independent public accountants, the review and discussion of periodic financial statements, and the evaluation and adoption of budgets.

Deloitte Haskins & Sells, Certified Public Accountants, have examined the accompanying financial statements and their opinion is included herein. Their examination includes a review of the systems of internal accounting control and appropriate tests of transactions. The auditors met with members of the Audit Committee to discuss the results of their examination, and were afforded an opportunity to present their opinions in the absence of management personnel with respect to various financial matters.

Exhibit 2.1 Statement of Management Responsibility for Financial Statements (Stauffer Chemical Company 1979 Annual Report, p. 23). Reprinted by permission.

include preparation of the statements, which is in fact done by the company's own staff (see Exhibit 2.1). Auditors are members of independent outside firms of accountants, who meet certain prescribed professional standards and have received a certificate or license to practice in the country or state of the client company. Although they perform the audit for a commercial fee which the company pays, it is important to note that it is their responsibility, not that of management, to decide how thorough a job is required, and thus companies cannot really negotiate the extent of auditing by insisting on a maximum fee payable.

AUDITORS' OPINION

Deloitte
Haskins + Sells
Certified Public Accountants
44 Montgomery Street
San Francisco, California

To the Stockholders of Stauffer Chemical Company:

We have examined the consolidated balance sheets of Stauffer Chemical Company and subsidiaries as of December 31, 1979 and 1978, and the related statements of consolidated earnings, consolidated stockholders' equity, and changes in consolidated financial position for the years then ended. Our examinations were made in accordance with generally accepted auditing standards and, accordingly, included such tests of the accounting records and such other auditing procedures as we considered necessary in the circumstances.

In our opinion, such consolidated financial statements present fairly the financial position of Stauffer Chemical Company and subsidiaries at December 31, 1979 and 1978, and the results of their operations and the changes in their financial position for the years then ended, in conformity with generally accepted accounting principles consistently applied during the period except for the change, with which we concur, in 1979 in the method of accounting for certain interest costs as described in the notes to financial statements.

Deloitte Haskins + Sells

February 19, 1980

Exhibit 2.2 Auditor's Opinion (Stauffer Chemical Company 1979 Annual Report, p. 34). Reprinted by permission.

All companies whose shares are listed on an organized stock exchange, and indeed many other companies too, have their financial statements audited, but it is suspected that few readers of these statements are aware of the exact limitations of an auditor's opinion. First of all, it is widely and incorrectly referred to as an Auditor's Certificate. It is in fact seldom a certificate. For instance, careful examination of the words used in the Typical U.S. auditor's opinion shown in Exhibit 2.2 will assure the reader that nothing has been certified as true or existing. All that is clear is that the auditors have conducted certain examinations of records and tests such as they considered necessary and that their opinion is that the three specified statements perform a definite function within a set of definite rules. There are four significant points to make here:

1. *The three statements which are audited are the balance sheet, the income statement, and the statement of changes in financial position.* The auditors do not comment on any other financial information that may be included in the annual report, although of course the notes to the three audited statements are covered by the opinion. It is conceivable therefore that some innocent readers of company reports believe the Chairman's remarks to have been verified by the auditors. This is understandably seldom the case.

2. *Fairness.* The words *present fairly* are used by design. There is a world of difference between presenting fairly and presenting accurately. Indeed, accounting often involves such judgments and estimates that accuracy, in the sense of 100% certainty, is impossible. Whereas a clock can be made accurate by reference to Greenwich mean time, accounting results cannot have such accuracy, since there are no absolute standards.

3. *GAAP.* What standards do exist for U.S. firms are known as Generally Accepted Accounting Principles, or GAAP. At the time of writing,

GAAP is expressed in a handbook of professional standards that runs to more than 2,000 pages. Even so, not all the accounting practices which are generally accepted by accounting firms are discussed in this volume, and not all practices can be verified by reference to these rules. Furthermore, GAAP sometimes changes more rapidly than the professional standards book can document. In countries where what is generally accepted is frequently not published in a handbook at all, it is that much more difficult to know the accepted standards.

Another drawback arises from the fact that what is a generally accepted reporting method in accounting practice may not be acceptable to a banker. Accounting cannot record all the assets or liabilities of a firm, since some have no definable monetary value. However, the banker regards certain unrecorded liabilities as very significant. For example, at the present time, U.S. balance sheets under GAAP do not show pension fund shortfall (that is, the actuarially computed value of vested benefits less the actuarially computed value of pension funds), although these are very significant. In the case of the Chrysler Corporation in 1978, for instance, this figure exceeded $1 billion, or more than one-third of its tangible net worth at that time.

4. *Consistency.* This means only that what was done last year has been done this year, not that the principles are themselves internally consistent, nor even that one subsidiary uses the same principles as another subsidiary. It does mean, however, that the figures are comparable one year with another.

QUALIFIED OPINIONS

No company likes a qualified opinion, neither does a banker or an investor. However, there are variations in the degree of qualification. If the opinion is stated "subject to . . ." some unresolved matter, that should be viewed differently from one that is stated "except for. . . ." The former (for example, "subject to the outcome of litigation") is used when there is an event outside the company's control that will affect certain recorded values of assets or liabilities. The latter (for example, "except for the change . . . in the method of accounting for certain interest costs," see Exhibit 2.2) is used where the auditor has to qualify an opinion either for a change in accounting policy that affects consistency (with which the auditor concurs or does not concur), or where GAAP is not followed (which is rare), or where a fair presentation is not made (which is even rarer). Before making such an opinion, the auditor will discuss the situation with the management of the company, and very often management will prefer to change the statements. This is especially true of statements that go to the U.S. Securities and Exchange Commission (namely, Form 10K), since that body will not accept any statements that are not in conformity with GAAP.[1]

[1]It should be observed that, in annual reports, U.S. companies may give shareholders less or even different financial information from that included in Form 10K.

WHO ARE THE AUDITORS?

Unfortunately for the banker, but fortunately for the accounting profession, not all practicing accountants belong to the largest and most respected auditing firms. Nor are these large firms, sometimes known as "The Big Eight," infallible, as many actions for negligence have shown. It falls to the banker, therefore, in whatever city he is, to know the reliability of the local accounting firms, and especially their integrity and independence. Small firms with large corporate clients are generally thought to be vulnerable to pressure from their clients which may erode their independence.

As an analyst, you should note whether the auditors have been changed. A change may not signify anything, but it could indicate that corporate management had a dispute over accounting policies with the previous auditors and sought a more congenial auditor.

Finally, a quick check of the date of the opinion will be worth the effort. The longer accounts take to prepare compared with the previous year, the more likely it is that there were unusual or complex transactions, or possible disagreements with auditors. Late accounts seldom contain good news.

SUMMARY OF SIGNIFICANT ACCOUNTING POLICIES

Consolidation

The consolidated financial statements include those of the Company and its subsidiaries. Investments in associated companies (20 to 50 per cent owned) are stated at cost plus equity in undistributed earnings since acquisition. All significant intercompany transactions and balances have been eliminated.

Marketable Securities

Marketable securities are stated at the lower of aggregate cost or market. Carrying value approximated market at December 31, 1979 and 1978.

Inventories

Inventories are stated at the lower of cost or market. Cost for domestic inventories is generally determined using the last-in, first-out method (LIFO). Cost for other inventories is determined using the average cost method.

Property, Plant and Equipment

Property, plant and equipment is stated at cost, which includes interest for fixed assets constructed during 1979. (See "Accounting Change" in accompanying notes.) Renewals and improvements are added to property. Maintenance and repairs are charged to income.

Depreciation is computed over the estimated useful lives of depreciable assets principally using the straight-line method. The estimated useful lives applied to principal properties vary from three to sixty years.

Any profit or loss related to the disposal or retirement of property is included in income.

Intangibles Arising from Business Acquisitions

Intangibles are amortized over periods up to forty years using the straight-line method, except for intangibles of $7 million acquired prior to November 1, 1970, which are not being amortized.

Income Taxes

The provision for income taxes is based on income reported for financial statement purposes rather than amounts currently payable under tax laws. Deferred taxes are provided for significant timing differences. Investment tax credits are reflected as a reduction of the provision for income taxes in the year the credits are available for tax purposes.

Earnings per Share

Earnings per common share is based on the weighted average number of shares of common stock outstanding. The computation excludes outstanding stock options, as their dilutive effect is not material.

Exhibit 2.3 Summary of Significant Accounting Policies (Stauffer Chemical Company 1979 Annual Report, p. 24). Reprinted by permission.

THE NATURE OF ACCOUNTING PRINCIPLES

After the auditor's opinion, a good next page to read is that setting out the summary of significant accounting principles (see Exhibit 2.3).

Although this is not a book on accounting, it will be important at this point to review some basic choices in accounting principles within GAAP that are available to management in presenting financial statements. In countries where accounting principles are less sophisticated than in the United States, it will pay to check through the list to see which ones are permissible and can thus be expected to influence the figures.

Skeptics have also described the list as "ways in which companies can make their income look good." It will be demonstrated later that the cashflow approach is the best for credit analysis, since changes in accounting principles cannot affect cashflow, except insofar as the current tax charge is greater or less.

Inventory

Inventory may be carried at last in first out (LIFO), first in first out (FIFO), or average cost. It is possible for a company to have some inventories at LIFO and some at FIFO. Different subsidiaries may have different policies. It is normal practice for a company to disclose the effect of inventory valuation in the notes to the financial statements.

Example 2.1. Stauffer Chemical Company reported in 1980 in the notes to their financial statement as follows: "Inventories stated using LIFO amounted to approximately 75 percent of total inventories at December 31, 1979 and 80 percent at December 31, 1978. If inventories stated at LIFO had been stated using the average cost method they would have been greater by approximately $100,300,000 at December 31, 1979 and $66,700,000 at December 31, 1978."

Actual inventories at December 31, 1979 were $318 million. Hence, the degree of undervaluation was on the order of 25–32%, depending on calculation basis. If the higher valuation had been used, cost of goods sold would have been lower (but it is not possible to estimate the amount) and thus trading profits would have been higher. On the other hand, cashflow would not have been affected (other than through the tax charge), as it is based on cash receipts less cash expenses for the period. In this case, the amount of cash spent on purchases of inventory and on manufacturing costs is unaffected by the method of inventory valuation.

Example 2.2. A brewing company carries its beer barrels in inventory at the lower of cost or market value. Market value is taken to be the cash deposit paid by the brewery's customers, which is refundable when they return the empty barrels. Suppose there are 10,000 barrels on hand, the cost of each barrel is $20, and the deposit charged is $5. Barrels are then carried at $5 each, making $50,000. If the deposit level is raised to $8, there will be a revaluation of inventory, giving rise to a pretax gain of $30,000, which will show up as extraordinary income. The cashflow effect of the revaluation will be none, although, of course, cash received and paid out for barrels will be greater. None of this, however, will affect income—that is, operating cash flow. Even if barrels are (illegally) retained by purchasers, this will give rise to an inventory write-off or noncash expense.

Fixed Assets and Depreciation

Any systematic and rational method of depreciation may be used. One must not forget that depreciation charges involve at least two estimates—namely, length of life and scrap value—and both of these are open to optimistic or pessimistic approaches. Neither, of course, affects cash flow (other than through current tax expense) since depreciation is noncash expense. Only purchases and sales of assets affect cash, and these are nonoperating items.

Changes in the method of depreciation or in the length of life of assets or the scrap value of those assets will significantly affect a firm's income. This is especially true for firms that are expanding. Normally, U.S. management can choose between straight-line depreciation or accelerated depreciation. Both methods will, of course, provide the same total expense over the life of the asset. However, because straight-line expense is lower in the early years, an expanding firm's income will appear greater if this method rather than accelerated depreciation is used.

Example 2.3. Suppose a company buys an asset worth $15,000 in 19X1, two of these in 19X2, 3 in 19X3, 4 in 19X4, 5 in 19X5. Accelerated depreciation will be, let's say, on the basis of $5,000 in 19X1, $4,000 in 19X2, $3,000 in 19X3, $2,000 in 19X4, and $1,000 in 19X5. This is the sum of the year's digits method with a five-year life. Annual depreciation charges will be as follows:

Year	Straight-Line	Accelerated
19X1	$3,000	$5,000
19X2	$6,000	$9,000 ($5,000 + $4,000)
19X3	$9,000	$12,000 ($5,000 + $4,000 + $3,000)
19X4	$12,000	$14,000 ($5,000 + $4,000 + $3,000 + $2,000)
19X5	$15,000	$15,000 ($5,000 + $4,000 + $3,000 + $2,000 + $1,000)
19X6	$15,000	$15,000

As a result, an expanding firm will prefer to show income after straight-line depreciation, as this will improve its position.

Notice how misleading it is to speak of cashflow as net income plus depreciation. This is discussed further in Chapter 3. For the present, it is enough to show that, if this firm in 19X2 had an income of $20,000 before depreciation and taxes, but after deducting every other expense, cashflow on a straight-line basis would be:

Income	$20,000
Depreciation	(6,000)
	14,000
Tax at 50%	(7,000)
Net Income	7,000
Cashflow	13,000

However, on an accelerated basis, cashflow would be:

Income	$20,000
Less depreciation	(9,000)
	11,000
Less tax at 50%	(5,500)
Net Income	5,500
Cashflow	14,500

How convenient life would be if companies could increase their cashflow by changing their depreciation policy. What has happened is indeed a lower tax charge, but whether cashflow has changed cannot be known without examining the degree to which cash payments have been made for taxes payable as well as for all revenue and expense items. This is discussed further in Chapter 3. Suffice it to say for the moment that cashflow is *not* net income plus depreciation, because this overlooks the effect of cash received or paid as a result of changes in the level of operating (working) assets and operating liabilities.

In some countries, fixed assets revaluation is practiced in such a way that, where professional outside valuers provide a market value substantially in excess of current recorded value for property, this new value is adopted, giving rise to an increase in owner's equity. Once again, this is noncash income and is normally shown in the reserve movements.

In many countries, costs of installation and development of properties are capitalized. (For example, interest expense on construction may be capitalized in the United States—see FASB No. 34.) This improves income but does not affect cashflow.

Revenue Recognition

The principle of revenue recognition probably gives rise to the greatest range in variation of reported income (see also Appendix to Chapter 10). It would be much easier for students of accounting if the phrase "revenue recognition" were replaced by "taking the profit" or some such words. After all, it is this question of recording the profit on a transaction which is at issue, and the issue essentially involves two things: timing and estimates.

Revenue on long-term contracts may normally be recognized on a completed contract basis or on a percentage of completion method. Under the former, no revenue or expense is shown until the contract is finished; under the latter, revenue is included proportionately with the percentage estimate of the total costs on the contract which have been incurred during that accounting period. The amount of cash received under the contract does not affect reported profits. Thus, we have both a timing question (Should no profit be shown in a period when no contracts are completed?) and an estimates question (Is it safe to report profit on a contract where only 15% of costs have been incurred and where our estimate of the remaining 85% may be very unreliable?).

Example 2.4. Far East shipyards had three contracts on hand during 19X9. The relevant details are as follows:

Ship Kristabel: Commenced in 19X7: Finished March 31, 19X9

Local contract price	$10,000,000
Cost of work in 19X7–19X8	8,400,000
Cost of work in 19X9	2,150,000
Percentage completed in 19X9	20%
Cash received	950,000

Ship Lara: Commenced in 19X8: Finished January 20, 19X9

Local contract price	3,000,000
Cost of work in 19X8	2,800,000
Cost of work in 19X9	390,000
Percentage completed in 19X9	5%
Cash received in 19X9	None

Ship Melina: Commenced May 1, 19X9

Total contract price	4,000,000
Cost of work in 19X9	1,250,000
Percentage completed	80%
Cash received	4,000,000

Assume there is $300,000 of unallocated central overhead. The completed contract method indicates a loss for the year of ($10,000,000 − $10,550,000)

+ ($3,000,000 − $3,190,000) + $300,000—or a loss of $1,040,000. On the other hand, the percentage of completion shows a profit of $1,260,000; this is (20% × 10,000,000) − $2,150,000 + (5% × $3,000,000) − $390,000 + (80% × $4,000,000) − $1,250,000 − $300,000)—Hence $1,260,000. Readers will note that the latter may be a "truer" picture if in fact, on contracts begun after April 19X9, price negotiation favored the shipyard and if in fact 80% is an accurate estimate of costs on the Melina. Also note the wide variation in reported income under the two different methods.

Other Examples

There are several other examples where the choice of accounting principle can affect reported net income. These include but are not limited to:

Cash discounts on sales may be recorded at the time of sale or at the time of collection.

Inventory costs may include storage costs, holding costs, and costs of acquiring inventories in addition to the normal purchase cost of goods.

Oil and gas exploration cost may be expensed, or it may be capitalized.

Intangible assets may be amortized over short or long lives.

Investment tax credits may be treated on the flow-through or deferred method.

Some subsidiaries may not be consolidated if they are regarded as significantly different from the parent company or "if the presentation of financial information concerning them would be more informative if made separately,"[2] and thus they are not considered when reporting the parent company's net income. This is typical of financing subsidiaries of manufacturing companies. In Germany, foreign subsidiaries are not consolidated at all but are carried on an equity basis. Although income would not necessarily be affected by the principles of consolidation, it could be very distorted if the equity method is not used.

The acquisition of companies can be treated on a pooling or purchase basis.

Pension liabilities may be calculated using a variety of different assumptions—for instance, the interest rate which is assumed to apply to the fund's earning assets. The related pension expense may be on either of two different conceptual bases. In 1981 in the case of General Motors Corporation, there was a change in the rate assumed which affected reported net earnings by several million dollars.

Various choices are available for recognizing revenue on purchasing or leasing operations.

[2]*GAAP Handbook*.

Various expenses relating to assets under construction may or may not be capitalized.

Warranty costs may be accrued at time of sale or expensed as incurred. Similarly, although estimated future losses should be provided for, in practice if the loss cannot be reasonably estimated, no provision is made. (For a special instance of this, see Manville Corporation's statements in 1980 and 1981.)

SPREADING FINANCIAL STATEMENTS

Armed with the knowledge of the limitations of audited figures, you can now proceed to the financial statements themselves. Companies are not obliged to present these in a rigidly defined format, and indeed under different national accounting systems, assets will sometimes be presented on the right hand side, sometimes on the left, and sometimes above or below the other side of the balance sheet.

As a result, bankers have developed a technique to transform this information into a standard pattern for the purpose of credit analysis. This technique is usually known as "spreading the figures." An example of a spread sheet is shown as Exhibit 2.4, but it is common practice for each bank to have variations based on local needs. (Another example is shown in the Appendix to this chapter.) Spread sheets are particularly useful in comparing a series of historical figures. They also impose a discipline on the analyst when calculating financial ratios. For example, the ratio earnings before interest and taxes/total assets is generally considered a very valuable ratio in showing the pretax rate of return generated by businesses in using assets.

Many analysts tend to start spreading the figures before reading the notes and the accounting policies. This is an unwise practice, since it can lead to classifying items incorrectly. For example, marketable securities are usually shown as current assets by companies and also by analysts on their spread sheets. On the other hand, some marketable securities may be described as "quoted investments." This may represent a long-term relationship between the subject company and another business. Most companies show this as a long-term asset, which should also be the credit analyst's approach, but occasionally such an investment might be shown by the company as a current asset, in which case the analyst should reclassify it.

Notes on Spreading Stauffer

For a good understanding of spreading, let's now work through the example shown as Exhibit 2.4 following the notes below:

1. *Balance Sheet* (Exhibit 2.5). No technical difficulties. Note only that some items have been combined on the bank spread sheet (for example, trade receivables and notes receivable) on the assumption that there is

NAME: STAUFFER CHEMICAL COMPANY (000'S OMITTED)

STATEMENT BASIS:
☒ CONSOLIDATED
☐ CO. ALONE

LINE	INCOME STATEMENT	DATE →	31/Dec/78	31/Dec/79		
1	NET SALES		1,328 114	1,526 160		
2	COST OF GOODS SOLD		(848 041)	(1,013 594)		
3	DEPRECIATION		(78 340)	(93 064)		
4	GROSS PROFIT		401 733	419 502		
5	OPERATING EXPENSES		135 883	161 866		
6	OPERATING PROFIT		265 080	257 636		
7	R&D		33 562	36 963		
8	INTEREST		37 923	31 839		
9	Other Expenses (Income)		6 432	(3 730)	Consider here the	
10	OTHER INCOME Interest Dividends		12 044	10 277	effects of accounting	
11	NET INCOME BEFORE TAXES		212 841	202 791	changes	
12	Minority Interest		10 206	16 555		
13	INCOME TAXES — CURRENT		48 464	24 418		
14	— DEFERRED		24 346	36 657		
15	NET INCOME		116 961	125 161		
16	Equity Earnings of Associates		9 054	10 800		
17	PREFERRED DIVIDENDS					
18	COMMON DIVIDENDS		42 600	47 132		
19	OTHER AFTER TAX DEDUCTIONS					
20						
21	ADDITION TO RETAINED EARNINGS		83 355	88 829		

Exhibit 2.4 Spread Sheet for Balance Sheet and Income Statement

STATEMENT BASIS:
☒ CONSOLIDATED
☐ CO. ALONE

NAME: **STAUFFER CHEMICAL COMPANY** (000'S OMITTED)

LINE	ASSETS	DATE →	31/Dec/78	31/Dec/79		
22	CASH		24 996	24 712		
23	MARKETABLE SECURITIES		64 011	31 191		
24	ACCOUNTS RECEIVABLE — NET		260 506	308 562		
25	INVENTORY		278 313	318 743		
26	OTHER CURRENT ASSETS		14 434	15 489		
27	**TOTAL CURRENT ASSETS**		642 260	698 697		
28	FIXED ASSETS, GROSS					
29	(DEPRECIATION)					
30	FIXED ASSETS — NET		903 246	1,040 542		
31	INVESTMENTS AND ADVANCES		40 384	41 412		
32	OTHER ASSETS		50 066	66 215		
33	INTANGIBLES		31 273	29 368		
34	**TOTAL**		1,667 229	1,876 234		

	LIABILITIES					
35	NOTES PAYABLE		135 841	196 699		
36	CURRENT PORTION — LONG TERM DEBT		13 599	9 145		
37	CURRENT PORTION — SUB. DEBT					
38	ACCOUNTS PAYABLE		97 106	116 857		
39	ACCRUED LIABILITIES		22 456	23 950		
40	ACCRUED TAXES		21 483	25 343		
41	OTHER		31 239	41 658		
42	**TOTAL CURRENT LIABILITIES**		321 724	413 652		
43	SENIOR LONG TERM DEBT		415 868	390 899		
44	**TOTAL UNSUBORDINATED LIABILITIES**		737 592	804 551		
45	SUBORDINATED DEBT					
46	**TOTAL LIABILITIES**					
47	DEFERRED TAXES		108 289	146 105		
48	OTHER RESERVES					
49	MINORITY INTEREST		60 011	74 433		
50	PREFERRED STOCK					
51	COMMON STOCK		55 757	55 856		
52	CAPITAL SURPLUS		95 936	96 703		
53	RETAINED EARNINGS		617 628	706 457		
54	(TREASURY STOCK)		(7 984)	(7 871)		
55	**TOTAL**		1,667 229	1,876 234		

Exhibit 2.4 *(Continued)*

56	WORKING CAPITAL		320,536	285,045		
57	CURRENT RATIO		2.0x	1.69x		
58	TNW + SUBORDINATED DEBT		730,064	821,777		
59	TOTAL UNSUB. LIAB. / CAPITAL BASE		1.01x	0.98x		
60	CAPITALIZED LEASES		None	None		
61	SOURCE OF FIGURES		A/R	A/R		
62	AUDITED/NON-AUDITED		Aud.	Aud.		

Exhibit 2.4 *(Continued)*

little real difference. This could be wrong; for instance, notes receivable might include funds arising from the sale of fixed assets. Without further information, one cannot say.

2. *Balance Sheet Ratios.* Note the drop in the current ratio and the drop in working capital. Tangible net worth (which is defined in the Glossary) has risen, but not enough to offset the rise in liabilities. At this stage, the analyst could expect to find later as an explanation of the change in working capital either a sharp drop in income from operations or a shortfall in capital expenditures compared with long-term sources of cash.
3. *Income Statement* (Exhibit 2.6). Note the considerable reclassifying of items on Exhibit 2.4. Depreciation was found from the notes to the balance sheet and has been taken out of Cost of Goods Sold. Research and Development (R&D) is shown after Operating Profit, since it is not related to sales volume, and Interest is excluded from Operating Expense, as it is a result of a financing decision, not an operating decision. The objective is to get a "clean" figure for Operating Profit (line 6) to compare with other companies in the same industry. Note also that Equity in Earnings of Associates (line 16) has been placed net of taxes below the Net Income line to show that it is noncash income and not connected with this company's operating profits.

DEALING WITH UNAUDITED STATEMENTS

If you have annual audited statements available to you, then the occasional unaudited statement between annual audits is acceptable. But bankers very often have to deal with totally unaudited statements drawn up by management. It is natural to wonder about their reliability given what you know about the nature of the auditing process. The only way that I can suggest using them with any degree of confidence is to perform for yourself some of the functions that the auditors perform. This may mean on occasion a physical inspection of the plant, inventory, and books of account. It almost certainly means asking management to spell out the basic accounting principles which have been used, paying particular attention to inventory valuation methods and the basis for recognizing revenue.

Which figures are likely to be the most reliable in unaudited statements? In general, liabilities will be fairly reliably stated since management has no reason to understate these and they can be checked in part by calls to other known lending institutions. Credit from suppliers is not so easy to check, so this figure may need to be taken on trust. Owner's equity should be treated as a residual number and left aside for the moment. Next you should examine assets, and these will be the hardest to check. In particular, inventory valuations are suspect, since they provide the easiest place to conceal the truth (see Chapter 6). Accounts receivable could be checked against an ageing

CONSOLIDATED BALANCE SHEET

Stauffer Chemical Company and Subsidiaries

ASSETS	December 31	1979	1978
		(Dollars in thousands)	
Current Assets	Cash	$ 24,712	$ 24,996
	Marketable Securities	31,191	64,011
	Receivables:		
	Trade — Net of Allowance for Doubtful Receivables (1979 — $2,963; 1978 — $2,554)	266,726	234,411
	Notes and Other	41,836	26,095
	Inventories:		
	Finished Products and Work in Progress	226,195	196,261
	Raw Materials and Supplies	92,548	82,052
	Prepaid Expenses	15,489	14,434
	Total Current Assets	**698,697**	**642,260**
Property, Plant and Equipment	Land	27,011	26,901
	Buildings, Machinery and Equipment — Net of Accumulated Depreciation (1979 — $600,925; 1978 — $527,852)	1,002,741	863,136
	Mineral Deposits — Net of Accumulated Depletion	10,790	13,209
	Property, Plant and Equipment — Net	**1,040,542**	**903,246**
Investments and Other Assets	Investments and Advances — Associated Companies	41,412	40,384
	Intangibles Arising from Business Acquisitions	29,368	31,273
	Other Assets	66,215	50,066
	Total Investments and Other Assets	**136,995**	**121,723**
	Total	**$1,876,234**	**$1,667,229**

See information on page 24 and notes to financial statements on pages 30 through 34.

Exhibit 2.5 Consolidated Balance Sheet, Stauffer Chemical Company and Subsidiaries

statement (see Chapter 6) to see if any uncollected accounts need to be written off. If the preceding year's financial statements have been audited or otherwise checked, it will be possible to check fixed assets against last year's figure. Beware of revaluations of fixed assets, and ask the borrower about depreciation policies. Also, in unaudited statements, it is safest to assume that any intangible assets have no value. Now it is possible to adjust owner's equity for any changes in asset values that you may feel necessary.

Next, examine carefully the income statement. Sales are more likely than expenses to be overstated, especially if revenue recognition methods are

LIABILITIES AND STOCKHOLDERS' EQUITY	December 31	**1979**	**1978**
		(Dollars in thousands)	
Current Liabilities	Notes Payable	$ 196,699	$ 135,841
	Accounts Payable	116,857	97,106
	Income Taxes Payable	17,899	15,121
	Accrued Interest	11,636	11,312
	Accrued Payroll	12,314	11,144
	Other Taxes Payable	7,444	6,362
	Other Liabilities	41,658	31,239
	Long-Term Debt Due within One Year	9,145	13,599
	Total Current Liabilities	**413,652**	**321,724**
Long-Term Debt		**390,899**	**415,868**
Deferred Income Taxes		**146,105**	**108,289**
Minority Interest in Subsidiaries		**74,433**	**60,011**
Stockholders' Equity	Common Stock, $1.25 Par — 70,000,000 Shares Authorized; Issued (1979 — 44,685,172; 1978 — 44,605,492); Outstanding (1979 — 43,882,583; 1978 — 43,791,426)	55,856	55,757
	Other Capital	96,703	95,936
	Retained Earnings	706,457	617,628
	Reacquired Common Shares — at Cost (1979 — 802,589; 1978 — 814,066)	(7,871)	(7,984)
	Stockholders' Equity — Net	**851,145**	**761,337**
	Total	**$1,876,234**	**$1,667,229**

(Stauffer Chemical Company 1979 Annual Report, pp. 26–27). Reprinted by permission.

being used that might be considered "creative accounting" (see Chapter 8). Watch out for shipments to customers on consignment which are treated as sales but which may be returned unsold later. Also, if you find items on the balance sheet such as "unbilled accounts receivable," then you should carefully inquire into when revenue is recognized, since such an item suggests that a profit has been recorded on items that have not even been invoiced to the customer. Since invoices invariably accompany deliveries, you can assume that this means there is inventory in the warehouse which is treated as sold even though it has been neither delivered nor invoiced to the customer.

STATEMENT OF CONSOLIDATED EARNINGS

Stauffer Chemical Company and Subsidiaries

		1979	1978
	Year ended December 31	(Dollars in thousands, except per-share amounts)	
Revenues	Net Sales	$1,526,160	$1,328,114
	Interest and Dividends	10,227	12,044
	Total Revenues	**1,536,387**	**1,340,158**
Cost and Expenses	Cost of Goods Sold	1,106,658	926,381
	Selling, General and Administrative	161,866	135,883
	Research and Development	36,963	33,562
	Interest	31,839	37,923
	Other Expense (Income) — Net	(3,730)	6,432
	Minority Interest	16,555	10,206
	Total Cost and Expenses	**1,350,151**	**1,150,387**
Earnings before Provision for Income Taxes		**186,236**	**189,771**
Provision for Income Taxes		**61,075**	**72,810**
Earnings from Consolidated Operations		**125,161**	**116,961**
Equity in Earnings of Associated Companies		**10,800**	**9,054**
Net Earnings		**$ 135,961**	**$ 126,015**
Earnings per Common Share		**$ 3.10**	**$ 2.88**

See information on page 24 and notes to financial statements on pages 30 through 34.

Exhibit 2.6 Statement of Consolidated Earnings, Stauffer Chemical Company and Subsidiaries (Stauffer Chemical Company 1979 Annual Report, p. 25). Reprinted by permission.

It is not likely that expenses have been understated. Borrowers may be using these financial statements as tax returns, so they will tend to be depressing income with a view to reducing taxes payable. Expenses might be overstated, but this would be to the lender's advantage since it would mean that income and cashflow were understated.

I cannot stress too strongly that knowledge of local practice as to how unaudited statements are made and used must be your guide in looking at them. In the United States, bankers tend to dismiss these statements as worthless, and they are right to do so since it is common knowledge that U.S. lenders expect audited statements. However, in many countries unaudited statements or tax returns are all that are available. They are better than nothing!

PROBLEMS

The end-of-chapter problems give you an opportunity to apply the material covered in each chapter. You will have to do additional research to solve some of the more advanced problems.

1. Why would a banker want to know why a borrower has changed auditors?
2. What would be likely to cause financial statements to be later than usual in being signed off by the accounting firm?
3. What is the meaning of *consistent* in the auditor's opinion?
4. What disciplines are applied in your country to auditing firms that provide financial statements?
5. In a country where the local currency has just been devalued against the U.S. dollar, a company which has long-term debt in U.S. dollars has adjusted its reported liability to reflect the increased amount payable in local currency. It has also adjusted upward the amount of the fixed asset (a factory) financed by this debt. Do you think this is reasonable? Why?
6. Changes in foreign exchange rates affect the value of all assets and liabilities of foreign subsidiaries, but parent companies do not always have to make adjustments for every change when preparing consolidated balance sheets.
   a. What choices are available to them in your country?
   b. How do movements in foreign exchange rates affect the parent company's cashflow? Is a loss shown on revaluing foreign subsidiaries a cash expense?
7. A manufacturing company which you are examining has an unconsolidated financing subsidiary. This subsidiary borrows from banks and other lenders to finance a portfolio of accounts receivable which arise from sales of products made by the parent company. The subsidiary gives its lenders the comfort of a support agreement from its parent which undertakes to maintain the subsidiary in a solvent condition. There are no other assets except cash, and no liabilities apart from banks and some currently payable taxes. Explain why such a company's debt should or should not be included as part of the consolidated parent company's debt for the purpose of ratio calculation.
8. Audited financial statements are offered to you as a lender, but the most recent ones are two years old. What would you do and why?
9. Give reasons why companies switch from FIFO to LIFO.

APPENDIX
ALTERNATIVE FORM OF SPREAD SHEET, INCORPORATING RATIOS AND CASHFLOWS

The simple form of spread sheet shown as Exhibit 2.4 has its limitations. A more useful form is shown in Exhibit 2.7, which includes ratio calculation and a cashflow analysis.

NOTES TO SPREAD SHEET

Comparative statement of financial condition:

Lines 1–8. Net Sales, Net Income, and certain key ratios.

Lines 9–22. Assets.

Lines 23–44. Liabilities and net worth.

Lines 45–53. State these numbers if available. Contingent Liabilities will probably not be on the balance sheet but in the notes, as will lease rentals.

Cashflow and ratio analysis:

Lines 54–68. Income statement items.

Lines 69–84. Calculation of cashflow from operations, as described in Chapter 3.

Lines 86–91. Sources of cash, other than operations.

Lines 92–98. Uses of cash, other than operations.

Lines 100–103. Useful ratios.

COMPARATIVE STATEMENT OF FINANCIAL CONDITION

NAME		SAMPLE COMPANY	**ADDRESS**				
AUDITOR		PRICE WATERHOUSE	**AMOUNTS IN**		MILLIONS	**CURRENCY**	US$
SOURCE — AUDIT OR DIRECT			AUDIT	AUDIT			
STATE IF QUALIFIED			NO	NO			
DATE (DAY/MO./YR.)			31 March 19X1	31 March 19X2			
LINE		**DESCRIPTION**	**AMOUNT**	**AMOUNT**	**AMOUNT**	**AMOUNT**	**AMOUNT**
1		**NET SALES**	719.8	770.2			
2		**NET INCOME**	19.8	16.7			
3		**WORKING CAPITAL**	135.5	128.3			
4		CURRENT RATIO	3.10x	2.77x			
5		QUICK ASSET RATIO	1.45x	1.27x			
6		**TANGIBLE NET WORTH**	201.1	210.5			
7		TOTAL LIABIL./TANG. NET WORTH	0.84x	0.79x			
8		TOTAL DEBT./TANG. NET WORTH	0.52x	0.46x			
9	ASSETS	CASH	9.8	4.6			
10		MARKETABLE SECURITIES	13.0	11.2			
11		RECEIVABLES/DEBTORS	68.7	76.5			
12		INVENTORY/STOCKS	104.8	106.3			
13							
14							
15		PREPAID EXPENSES	2.5	3.0			
16		**TOTAL CURRENT ASSETS**	198.8	201.6			
17		NET FIXED ASSETS	158.2	163.5			
18		INV. & ADV. SUBS & AFFILIATES	12.7	12.6			
19							
20							
21		INTANGIBLES	25.2	23.7			
22		**TOTAL ASSETS**	394.9	401.4			

Exhibit 2.7 Alternative Spread Sheets

23	LIABILITIES	SHORT-TERM DEBT	6.6	12.8			
24		ACCOUNTS PAYABLE/CREDITORS	48.6	54.2			
25		ACCRUALS					
26		INCOME TAXES	8.1	5.7			
27							
28							
29		**TOTAL CURRENT LIABILITIES**	63.3	72.7			
30							
31							
32		**TOTAL LONG-TERM SENIOR DEBT**	97.8	53.3			
33							
34							
35		**TOTAL Subordinated long-term Debt**					
36		Deferred Tax	7.5	5.6			
37		OTHER L.T. Liability	—	5.6			
38		**TOTAL L.T. Liabilities & Reserves**	105.3	94.5			
39		PREFERRED STOCK/SHARES	19.5	18.5			
40		COMMON STOCK/Ordinary Shares	45.0	47.3			
41		CAPITAL SURPLUS/Capital Reserves					
42		EARNED SURPLUS/Retained Earnings	164.0	170.6			
43			(2.2)	(2.2)			
44		**TOTAL LIABILITIES & Net Worth**	394.9	401.4			
45	**LEASE RENTALS**						
46	**CONTINGENT LIABILITIES**						
47	**Inventory**	FINISHED GOODS					
48		WORK IN PROCESS					
49		RAW MATERIALS, ETC.					
50	**Fixed Assets**	LAND AND BUILDINGS					
51		MACHINERY, Equipment, etc.					
52		GROSS FIXED ASSETS	279.8	285.8			
53		DEPRECIATION RESERVE	121.6	122.3			

CASH FLOW
RATIO ANALYSIS
NAME SAMPLE COMPANY

	DATE	31 March 19X1		31 March 19X2							
	No. OF MONTHS	12		12							
LINE	DESCRIPTION	AMOUNT	%	AMOUNT	%	AMOUNT	%	AMOUNT	%	AMOUNT	%
54	**NET SALES (GROWTH RATE)**	719.8		770.2	7.0						
55	COST OF GOODS SOLD (% OF SALES)	531.9	73.9	573.4	74.4						
56	GROSS OPERATING PROFIT (% OF SALES)	187.9	26.1	196.8	25.6						
57	SELLING, GEN., ADMIN. EXP. (% OF SALES)	128.1	17.8	134.7	17.5						
58	Operating Profit (% of Sales)	59.8	8.3	62.1	8.1						
59	DEPRECIATION (% AVG. GROSS PLANT)	13.5		14.4	5.1						
60	OTHER NON-CASH CHARGES										
61	OTHER INCOME (% OF SALES)										
62	OTHER EXPENSE (% OF SALES)										
63	Profit before Int. & Other Fixed Chgs. (% of Sales)	46.3	6.4	47.7	6.2						
64	INT. & OTHER FIXED CHGS: (% Avg. Debt)	6.9		7.3	7.3						
65	Profit Before Income Tax (% of Sales)	39.4	5.5	40.4	5.2						
66	INCOME TAX (% PRE-TAX PROFIT)	19.6	49.7	19.0	47.0						
67	EXTRAORDINARY CHARGES			5.1							
68	**NET INCOME (% OF SALES)**	19.8	2.8	16.3	2.1						

Exhibit 2.7 *(Continued)*

Line	Section	Item										
69	NET-OPERATING CASH GENERATION	NET INCOME			16.3							
70		DEPRECIATION			14.4							
71		OTHER NON-CASH CHARGES			7.1							
72		**GROSS FUNDS FROM OPERATIONS**			37.8							
73		LESS CHANGES IN NET WORKING ASSETS										
74												
75		(INC.)/DEC. IN ACCOUNTS RECEIVABLE — %		9.5	(7.8)	9.9						
76		(INC.)/DEC. INVENTORY INV./COST OF GOODS SOLD — %		19.7	(1.5)	18.5						
77		(INC.)/DEC. PREPAID EXPENSES PPD. EXPS./COST OF GOODS SOLD — %			(0.5)							
78												
79												
80		INC./(DEC.) ACCTS. PAYABLE ACCTS: PAY./COST OF GOODS SOLD — %		9.1	5.6	9.5						
81		INC./(DEC.) TAXES PAYABLE TAXES PAY./PREV. INC. TAX — %			(4.3)							
82		INC./(DEC.) ACCRUALS ACCRUALS/TOTAL OPER. EXP. — %										
83		Sub-Total: Change in NWA			(8.5)							
84		**TOTAL (LINE 72 + 83) CASH FROM OPS**			29.3							
85	NON-OPERATING CASH GENERATION	SALE OF EQUITY			1.3							
86		INC. LONG-TERM DEBT										
87		INC. SHT.-TERM DEBT (and Bills Dis.)			6.2							
88		SALE OF ASSETS										
89		SALE OF MARKETABLE SECURITIES										
90												
91		TOTAL			7.5							

Line	Section	Item										
92	NON-OPERATING CASH NEEDS	CAPITAL EXPEND. — GROSS SALES /GROSS PLANT (LAND, BLDG., EQUIP)		257.3	19.7	264.5						
93		DIVIDENDS PAID (Payout Ratio)			9.7	59.5						
94		RED. LONG-TERM DEBT			14.5							
95		RED. SHORT-TERM DEBT (and bills dis.)										
96		INV. & ADV. SUBS'. AND AFFIL.			(0.1)							
97												
98		TOTAL			43.8							
99	NET INC./(DEC.) IN CASH AND MARKETABLE SECURITIES (LINE 84 + 91 MINUS LINE 98)				(7.0)							
100	Analytical Ratios	NET PROFIT/NET WORTH		9.8		7.9						
101		EBIT/Total Assets		14.8		15.0						
102		DEBT SERVICE COVERAGE										
103		NWA/Sales										

Exhibit 2.7 *(Continued)*

3 Cashflow Analysis

This chapter explains how to perform a cashflow analysis and how to find cash from operations. Bearing in mind that companies normally provide financial statements based on accrual accounting, together with a statement of changes in working capital (that misleading document sometimes called the funds flow statement), you must once again put on your detective's hat. Your main task will be to distinguish first between cash and noncash revenues and expenses, and then to distinguish between operating and nonoperating items.

Cashflow analysis is necessary because of the flexibility in accounting policies and because financial statements are prepared from the point of view of recording income and presenting information to investors. Modern credit analysis is based on a return to business fundamentals (see Chapter 1). No banker was ever repaid out of accrual income—hence the concentration on cashflow. Further, a cashflow statement is intended to provide some basis for estimating the future ability of the business to generate cash—hence the emphasis on repeatable operating performance and the exclusion of "once and for all" gains and losses.

While income and profitability is important, solvency (that is, the ability to pay one's debts) is of vital short-term interest to the banker. In fact, as will be seen in Chapter 5, there is strong evidence that cashflow/total liabilities is one of the most important financial ratios in predicting future problem credits.

Our purpose will therefore be to make a summary statement of sources and uses of cash for the year under review so that the following questions can be answered:

1. Did the business generate positive cash flows after allowing for the effects of changes in the working accounts?
2. How was capital expenditure financed?
3. What use was made of debt raised?

Some simple cashflow examples now follow. Later in the chapter, a more difficult cashflow is shown.

NET WORKING ASSETS

Before beginning, it is necessary to introduce one new concept. While importance has traditionally been given to working capital, it is now considered necessary to refine this, since there are often items included in current assets or current liabilities which are not related to normal operations. For instance, the payment of dividends is a result of financial decision making, and although dividends payable is a current liability, it is not regarded as a working account. So, too, maturing long-term debt items are not considered as working accounts.

Thus, a new net current item called net working assets (NWA) is used as a substitute for working capital. This can be defined as those items (assets or liabilities) which move with the level of sales, in particular accounts receivable, accounts payable, and inventories (including work in progress). It does not include cash or short-term debt, as the objective of this exercise is to find the cash or lack of it resulting from the ordinary process of buying raw materials, manufacturing these into products, selling them, and collecting the proceeds. The result of this process or cycle is called cash from operations.

Example 3.1. Let's begin with the simplest example, drawn from a story on management training once told to me by a successful businessman in retail ladies' fashion. According to Maurice, management training for his shop managers involved giving them a stall in a street market and $200. "Go away," he used to say, "and run that stall in the market. Buy dresses for $1 and sell for $3. But bring me more cash at the end of the week than you started with, and no dresses!" The point to be learned is this: Net working assets consists here of only one thing—namely, the inventory of dresses. Suppose sales of dresses during the week were $3,000 (all cash) and purchases were $1,400. If at the end of the week the trainee has 400 unsold dresses at $1 each (cash price), his profit, of which he will be very proud, is clearly:

Sales	$3,000
Less purchases	(1,400)
Less closing inventory	(400)
= Cost of goods sold	1,000
Profit	$2,000

His cash from operations (that is, the cash he has left to give back to Maurice) is, however, only $1,600 plus the $200 that he began with. The difference between the profit of $2,000 and the $1,600 cash generated represents the amount of unsold dresses—the one thing Maurice did not want because who knows what those dresses will fetch next week?

Example 3.2. Alan runs an engineering job shop that performs subcontracts for various local firms. He employs eight people and always has a lot of work going on. Three months' figures are available, disclosing the following information:

	Beginning Balances: February 1, 19X0	Ending Balances: April 30, 19X0
Inventories	$ 960	$ 1,430
Work in progress	1,425	1,960
Accounts receivable	2,400	4,175
Accounts payable	(853)	(1,042)
Accrued expenses	(460)	(745)
Net working assets	3,472	5,778
Cash	250	350
Plant and machines	6,400	6,000
Total net assets	10,122	12,128

Three months to April 30: Sales	$4,000
Cost of goods sold	(1,500)
Depreciation	(400)
Other Expenses	(94)
Profit before tax	2,006

Cash from operations, however, is not so easily found, and we must first perform a simple transaction analysis, recording the sales and expenses as follows:

	Assets			
	Cash	Net Working Assets	Plant	Liabilities and Owner's Equity
February 1, 19X0	$ 250	$ 3,472	$6,400	$ 10,122
1. Sales		+4,000		+4,000
2. Cost of goods sold		(1,500)		(1,500)
3. Depreciation			(400)	(400)
4. Other expenses		(94)		(94)
5. Cash from operations	+100	(100)		
April 30, 19X0	350	5,778	6,000	12,128

Explanation:

Line 1. Notice that any change in assets is matched by a change on the side of Liabilities and Owner's Equity. Sales were on account, so they must have increased accounts receivable (that is, made net working assets increase).

Line 2. Cost of goods sold makes inventory and work in progress decrease. Hence, net working assets decrease.

Line 3. Depreciation is a noncash expense; it makes plant go down, and thus does not affect net working assets.

Line 4. Other expenses are going to make accrued expenses increase. Hence, net working assets go down.

Line 5. Since we do not know exactly what cash collections or what payments in cash were made, we have to deduce the net figure. Sales make accounts receivable go up (net working assets goes up); expenses incurred (lines 2 and 4) make net working assets go down. Hence, cash collections decrease net working assets, and cash paid to settle liabilities increases net working assets since it reduces the liability. Thus, the balancing figure, which is cash from operations, will be the net of these payments and collections. This turns out to be $100—very different from profits of $2,006!

Note also that we could have found cash from operations by taking net income, adding back noncash charges (in this case only depreciation of $400), and subtracting the change in net working assets. Thus, $2,006 + $400 − ($5,778 − $3,472) = $100. Observe that the popular notion of cashflow being net income plus depreciation is true *only* if there is no change from beginning to ending net working assets. Given that net working assets normally rise with inflation and business activity, this assumption will generally be true only by accident.

Compare this result with the effect on working capital. Beginning balance for working capital was $3,472 + $250 = $3,722 and ending balance is $6,128. Under the conventional approach this is a good sign—working capital has gone up nearly 70%. But beware! There is no provision for current taxes, and even a small change in ability to collect receivables will make this business into one where profits are good but cash decreases. Thus, with Alan's Engineering Company, we have a strong expansion but a shortage of cash and an increasing lack of solvency. Any shortfall in the recorded value of work in progress compared with its salable value will impair this solvency even further.

Sometimes a business goes through a period of rapid growth and high profitability and also experiences a mounting need for cash. Such an example is Wonderdrug Company, which has, let's say, discovered a cure for the common cold. Sales were growing 40% in 19X0 and 19X1. What is likely to happen to cash from operations? How can this growth be financed? Is a pretax profit margin of about 16% going to be enough to generate internal cash for expansion? How do we show capital expenditure in a cashflow analysis?

Before working through the example, let's make one more definition clear. Cash from operations is the cash resulting from buying, manufacturing, selling, and collecting the proceeds; there is also another term, Funds from Operations (FFO). This is an accrual accounting concept—it is not the same as cash from operations and is defined as: sales (accounting basis) minus cost of goods sold and other cash-related operating expenses (accounting basis), or net income plus noncash expenses. In order to find cash from operations, it is necessary to find funds from operations and then add or subtract the change in net working assets.

Example 3.3. We are now ready to perform the 19X9 transaction analysis for Wonderdrug Company using data shown in Exhibit 3.1.

Exhibit 3.1 Wonderdrug Company (in thousands of dollars)

	19X8	19X9	19X0
Cash	$ 9	$ 15	$ 25
Inventory	210	295	436
Accounts Receivable	240	336	470
Net Plant	400	525	650
	859	1,171	1,581
Accounts Payable	126	177	247
Accrued Expenses	100	143	201
Short-Term Debt	83	181	353
Owner's Equity	550	670	780
	859	1,171	1,581
Sales	1,714	2,400	3,360
Cost of Goods Sold	1,028	1,440	2,016
Selling General and Administrative Expense	257	360	420
Depreciation	88	125	175
Research and Development	100	136	190
Earnings before Taxes	241	339	559
Taxes	(120)	(169)	(279)
Net Income	121	170	280
Dividends	50	50	70
Retained Earnings	70	120	210
Net Working Assets	224	311	458
Working Capital	150	145	130
Capital Expenditure	224	250	300

First set out the beginning and ending balances. Then enter items from the income statement under each column—for example, sales increases owner's equity and also increases accounts receivable; cost of goods sold decreases owner's equity and increases accrued expenses (which means it decreases net working assets).

To perform the 19X9 transaction analysis for Wonderdrug Company we use the figures shown in Exhibit 3.1:

	Cash	Net Working Assets	Plant	Short-Term Debt	Owner's Equity
December 31, 19X8	$ 9	$ 224	$ 400	$ 83	$ 550
Sales		+2,400			+2,400
Cost of goods sold		(1,440)			(1,440)
Selling general and administrative expense		(360)			(360)
Depreciation			(125)		(125)
Research and development		(136)			(136)
Taxes		(169)			(169)
Dividends	(50)				(50)
New short-term debt	+98			+98	
New plant	(250)		250		
Cash from operations	208	(208)			
December 31, 19X9	15	311	525	181	670

Sources and Uses of Cash 19X9

Cash from operations	$208	Buy plant	$250
New debt	98	Pay dividends	50
	306		300
		Increase in cash	6
			306

Only two new points are introduced here: capital expenditure and dividends paid. By convention, all capital expenditure is treated as being made for cash. The reason is that accounts payable are for trade purchases unless the company tells you otherwise. Dividends too are paid in cash. In the absence of a dividends payable liability, these are also put through the cash column.

Observations

Although net working assets expanded from 224 to 331 (+38%), funds from operations was strong at 295, thanks to the substantial profitability of sales. Thus, cash from operations was positive at 208. However, because of the 40% sales growth, a substantial amount of capital expenditure was required. Cash from operations less dividends paid provided 158 toward capital expenditure, and the remainder had to be financed by new debt of 98. This would have decreased working capital substantially but for the strong profit performance. In fact, working capital falls by 5, while net working assets increase by 87.

It might appear that the increase in new working assets is being financed by debt, but this would be a wrong interpretation. As cash from operations is positive, the absence of capital expenditure would have meant that no new debt was required. Here a short-term source of cash is being used to finance a long-term need (capital expenditure) under the guise of financing higher inventories and receivables. If growth continues at 40% with corresponding increases in capital expenditure, this debt will never be repaid.

Net Working Assets/Sales

Notice that a useful ratio to calculate is net working assets/sales. This indicates whether the terms of trade (credit given and credit taken) have changed and whether inventories are in about the same proportion to sales as in the previous year. Here for 19X9 the net working assets/sales ratio is 13.0%, which compares favorably with 13.1% in 19X8. If inventories expanded without an equal increase in accounts payable or accrued liabilities, the net working assets/sales ratio would increase—or in fact get worse from the point of view of cash, as higher ending net working assets means less cash from operations. Wonderdrug is fortunate, perhaps because of the high added value in production, that its net working assets/sales ratio is only 13%. Many other companies have net working assets/sales ratios around 20%. This favorable ratio explains why growth at 40% produces less strain on Wonderdrug than one would expect.

Assume the same sales growth, but a 20% net working assets/sales ratio:

Beginning net working assets (20% of 19X8 sales of 1,714)	$342.8
Ending net working assets (20% of 19X9 sales of 2,400)	480.0
19X9 increase in net working assets	137.2

Immediately it is clear that cash from operations would be 295 − 137.2 = 157.8 instead of 208, leading to a new debt requirement of 148.2 in place of 98. In the following year, the effect would be:

Beginning net working assets	480.0
Ending net working assets (20% of 3,360)	672.0
19X0 increase in NWA	192.0

This will lead to cash from operations of 455 − 192.0 = 263 and new debt of 217, producing total debt at the end of 19X0 of 83 + 148.2 + 217 = 448.2. By this point, working capital has nearly disappeared and anything wrong with inventory will severely impair solvency. Hence, rapid growth even with good profitability can be risky for a lender.

Another approach to Wonderdrug's current asset/current liability situation parallels the net working assets/sales ratio. This involves calculating the number of days represented by receivables, payables, and inventory figures.

Thus for 19X9, number of days of inventory on hand at December 31, 19X9 is:

$$\frac{\text{Inventory}}{\text{Cost of goods sold}} \times 365$$

That is,

$$\frac{295}{1{,}440} \times 365 = 74.78 \text{ days}$$

Number of days of receivables on hand is:

$$\frac{\text{Receivables}}{\text{Sales}} \times 365$$

That is,

$$\frac{336}{2{,}400} \times 365 = 51.1 \text{ days}$$

while payables are:

$$\frac{\text{Payables}}{\text{Costs of goods sold}} \times 365$$

That is,

$$\frac{177}{1{,}440} \times 365 = 44.8 \text{ days}$$

The cash cycle is therefore said to be: Inventory (days) + accounts receivable (days) − payables (days):

$$74.78 + 51.1 - 44.8 = 81.08 \text{ days}$$

This can be compared to the 19X8 figures, which turn out to be:

$$74.56 + 50.98 - 44.73 = 80.81 \text{ days}$$

The net working assets/sales method is considered superior to the current asset/current liability approach, as it will include such items as accrued expenses, prepayment, and other current assets or liabilities related to operations.

In general, the analyst is advised to check any variation in the net working assets/sales ratio by seeing what changes there are in days of inventory, days of payables, or days of receivables. These points are discussed further in Chapter 6.

NONOPERATING ITEMS

Nonoperating items are those revenues or expenses that are not related to day-to-day business transactions. Obviously, sales and purchases of goods are operating items. The payment of current taxes is also considered part of the normal cycle of operations. However, capital expenditure, dividend payments, acquisitions, and raising of new capital are definitely nonoperating items. We have to exclude these carefully in constructing a cashflow analysis because we want to find cash from operations—that is, the cash generated in the day-to-day cycle of the business that we can reasonably expect (other things being equal) to be repeated next year.

Because nonoperating items are not directly related to the level of sales, they are considered to be more subject to management control than are operating items. Capital expenditure, for instance, can usually be postponed. Dividend payments can be reduced or omitted. But the regular process of buying goods, manufacturing, paying for purchases, selling goods, and collecting the proceeds of sales is the life blood of the business—hence, our interest in cash from operations, as that is the source of repayment toward which the banker most regularly looks.

HOW TO COMPLETE A TRANSACTION ANALYSIS

There are many nonoperating items besides capital expenditure and dividends. Rather than giving a comprehensive list of these, it will be more constructive to work through an example. The way in which this is done is called a transaction analysis, since it emphasizes treating each transaction separately so as to find its effect upon cash. What you do is use published financial statements, together with the associated notes. By using the beginning balance sheet, the income statement, and the ending balance sheet, you can convert accrual accounting information into cashflow information. How this is done is now explained using an actual example.

CONSOLIDATED BALANCE SHEET

Stauffer Chemical Company and Subsidiaries

ASSETS	December 31	1979	1978
		(Dollars in thousands)	
Current Assets	Cash	$ 24,712	$ 24,996
	Marketable Securities	31,191	64,011
	Receivables:		
	Trade — Net of Allowance for Doubtful Receivables (1979 — $2,963; 1978 — $2,554)	266,726	234,411
	Notes and Other	41,836	26,095
	Inventories:		
	Finished Products and Work in Progress	226,195	196,261
	Raw Materials and Supplies	92,548	82,052
	Prepaid Expenses	15,489	14,434
	Total Current Assets	**698,697**	**642,260**
Property, Plant and Equipment	Land	27,011	26,901
	Buildings, Machinery and Equipment — Net of Accumulated Depreciation (1979 — $600,925; 1978 — $527,852)	1,002,741	863,136
	Mineral Deposits — Net of Accumulated Depletion	10,790	13,209
	Property, Plant and Equipment — Net	**1,040,542**	**903,246**
Investments and Other Assets	Investments and Advances — Associated Companies	41,412	40,384
	Intangibles Arising from Business Acquisitions	29,368	31,273
	Other Assets	66,215	50,066
	Total Investments and Other Assets	**136,995**	**121,723**
	Total	**$1,876,234**	**$1,667,229**

See information on page 24 and notes to financial statements on pages 30 through 34.

Exhibit 3.2 Consolidated Balance Sheet and Statement of Consolidated Earnings, Stauffer Chemical Company and Subsidiaries (Stauffer Chemical Company 1979 Annual Report, pp. 25, 26, 27). Reprinted by permission.

Example 3.4. Balance sheets, income statement, Statement-of-Changes in Consolidated Financial Position, and notes relating to Stauffer Chemical Company's 1979 annual results are shown as Exhibits 3.2 and 3.3. First, set out the balances as shown in Exhibit 3.4, with assets on the left and liabilities

LIABILITIES AND STOCKHOLDERS' EQUITY	December 31	1979	1978
		(Dollars in thousands)	
Current Liabilities	Notes Payable	$ 196,699	$ 135,841
	Accounts Payable	116,857	97,106
	Income Taxes Payable	17,899	15,121
	Accrued Interest	11,636	11,312
	Accrued Payroll	12,314	11,144
	Other Taxes Payable	7,444	6,362
	Other Liabilities	41,658	31,239
	Long-Term Debt Due within One Year	9,145	13,599
	Total Current Liabilities	**413,652**	**321,724**
Long-Term Debt		**390,899**	**415,868**
Deferred Income Taxes		**146,105**	**108,289**
Minority Interest in Subsidiaries		**74,433**	**60,011**
Stockholders' Equity	Common Stock, $1.25 Par — 70,000,000 Shares Authorized; Issued (1979 — 44,685,172; 1978 — 44,605,492); Outstanding (1979 — 43,882,583; 1978 — 43,791,426)	55,856	55,757
	Other Capital	96,703	95,936
	Retained Earnings	706,457	617,628
	Reacquired Common Shares — at Cost (1979 — 802,589; 1978 — 814,066)	(7,871)	(7,984)
	Stockholders' Equity — Net	**851,145**	**761,337**
	Total	**$1,876,234**	**$1,667,229**

Exhibit 3.2 *(Continued)*

STATEMENT OF CONSOLIDATED EARNINGS

Stauffer Chemical Company and Subsidiaries

		Year ended December 31	1979	1978
			(Dollars in thousands, except per-share amounts)	
Revenues	Net Sales		$1,526,160	$1,328,114
	Interest and Dividends		10,227	12,044
		Total Revenues	**1,536,387**	**1,340,158**
Cost and Expenses	Cost of Goods Sold		1,106,658	926,381
	Selling, General and Administrative		161,866	135,883
	Research and Development		36,963	33,562
	Interest		31,839	37,923
	Other Expense (Income) — Net		(3,730)	6,432
	Minority Interest		16,555	10,206
		Total Cost and Expenses	**1,350,151**	**1,150,387**
Earnings before Provision for Income Taxes			**186,236**	**189,771**
Provision for Income Taxes			**61,075**	**72,810**
Earnings from Consolidated Operations			**125,161**	**116,961**
Equity in Earnings of Associated Companies			**10,800**	**9,054**
Net Earnings			**$ 135,961**	**$ 126,015**
Earnings per Common Share			**$ 3.10**	**$ 2.88**

See information on page 24 and notes to financial statements on pages 30 through 34.

Exhibit 3.2 *(Continued)*

STATEMENT OF CHANGES IN CONSOLIDATED FINANCIAL POSITION

Stauffer Chemical Company and Subsidiaries

	Year ended December 31	1979	1978
		(Dollars in thousands)	
Source of Working Capital	Operations:		
	Net Earnings	$135,961	$126,015
	Depreciation	93,064	78,340
	Deferred Income Taxes	37,816	23,689
	Other — Net	18,645	4,616
	Provided from Operations	**285,486**	**232,660**
	Issuance of Long-Term Debt	9,475	9,736
	Issuance of Common Stock	979	1,353
	Property Disposals	6,125	5,474
	Total Source	**302,065**	**249,223**
Application of Working Capital	Capital Expenditures	239,303	201,196
	Dividends Paid	47,132	42,660
	Reduction of Long-Term Debt	34,444	10,867
	Acquisition — Net Non-Current Assets		18,715
	Other — Net	16,677	7,431
	Total Application	**337,556**	**280,869**
Decrease in Working Capital		**$ (35,491)**	**$ (31,646)**
Change in Working Capital by Component	Cash and Marketable Securities	$ (33,104)	$ (7,777)
	Receivables	48,056	48,300
	Inventories	40,430	44,614
	Prepaid Expenses	1,055	1,517
	Notes Payable	(60,858)	(112,451)
	Accounts Payable	(19,751)	(7,470)
	Income Taxes Payable	(2,778)	15,501
	Other Current Liabilities	(8,541)	(13,880)
	Decrease in Working Capital	**$ (35,491)**	**$ (31,646)**

See information on page 24 and notes to financial statements on pages 30 through 34.

Exhibit 3.3 Funds Flow Statement and Notes (Stauffer Chemical Company 1979 Annual Report, pp. 28–34). Reprinted by permission.

NOTES TO FINANCIAL STATEMENTS

Stock Split

In May, 1979, the stockholders approved an increase in authorized shares of common stock from 30,000,000 shares to 70,000,000 shares, a two-for-one stock split, and a reduction in par value from $2.50 to $1.25 per share. Common stock data in the accompanying consolidated financial statements and notes to financial statements have been restated for the two-for-one stock split.

Accounting Change

During the fourth quarter of 1979, the Company adopted Financial Accounting Standards Board Statement No. 34, "Capitalization of Interest Cost," which requires that interest be added to the cost of qualifying assets. Interest cost during 1979 was $44,454,000, of which $12,615,000 was capitalized. The effect of capitalizing such interest was to increase net earnings by $6,417,000 or $.15 per share. Previously reported results for the first three quarters of 1979 have been restated as follows:

	As Previously Reported		Accounting Change		As Restated	
	Net Earnings	Per Share	Net Earnings	Per Share	Net Earnings	Per Share
	(Net earnings in thousands)					
Quarter Ended:						
March 31	$61,253	$1.40	$ 949	$.02	$62,202	$1.42
June 30	23,597	.54	1,356	.03	24,953	.57
September 30	11,013	.25	1,867	.05	12,880	.30

Inventories

Inventories stated using LIFO amounted to approximately 75 per cent of total inventories at December 31, 1979, and 80 per cent at December 31, 1978. If inventories stated at LIFO had been stated using the average cost method they would have been greater by approximately $100,300,000 at December 31, 1979, and $66,700,000 at December 31, 1978.

Income Taxes

The provision for income taxes includes the following:

	1979	1978
	(Dollars in thousands)	
Current:		
Federal	$ 12,886	$ 34,866
State	7,094	8,227
Foreign	4,438	5,371
	24,418	**48,464**
Deferred:		
Depreciation	27,041	24,665
Capitalized interest	6,090	
Other	3,526	(319)
	36,657	**24,346**
Total	**$ 61,075**	**$ 72,810**

A reconciliation of the provision for income taxes and the effective tax rate with the amount computed by applying the federal statutory income tax rate follows:

	1979 Amount	1979 Rate	1978 Amount	1978 Rate
	(Dollars in thousands)			
Income taxes computed at statutory rate	$85,669	46%	$91,090	48%
State tax, net of federal income tax	3,831	2	4,278	2
Investment tax credits	(19,685)	(10)	(16,395)	(9)
Percentage depletion	(7,858)	(4)	(7,334)	(4)
Lower foreign tax rates	(10,473)	(6)	(2,956)	(2)
Minority interest	7,615	4	4,899	3
Other — net	1,976	1	(772)	
Provision and effective tax rate	**$61,075**	**33%**	**$72,810**	**38%**

The net amount of prepaid income taxes related to current timing differences, included in prepaid expenses, was $9,800,000 at December 31, 1979 and $8,700,000 at December 31, 1978.

Deferred taxes have not been provided on undistributed earnings of consolidated domestic and foreign subsidiaries as such earnings will be required in the subsidiaries' operations. The cumulative amount of these earnings on which United States taxes have not been provided was $124,800,000 at December 31, 1979. Under current federal income tax laws, dividend exclusions and foreign tax credits would be available to reduce substantially the federal income taxes which might otherwise result from distributions of such undistributed accumulated earnings. The estimated income taxes payable on these earnings, if distributed, would be $17,900,000 at December 31, 1979.

Exhibit 3.3 *(Continued)*

Notes Payable

	1979	1978
	(Dollars in thousands)	
Commercial paper	$178,170	$ 67,998
Other notes payable	18,529	67,843
Total	**$196,699**	**$135,841**
Average interest rate at year-end	13%	10%
Maximum aggregate notes payable outstanding at any month-end during the year	$196,699	$135,841
Average month-end notes payable outstanding during the year	$ 93,846	$ 37,113
Weighted average interest rate for the year	11%	8%

The Company had unused short-term bank lines of credit amounting to $54,700,000 at December 31, 1979.

Long-Term Debt

	1979	1978
	(Dollars in thousands)	
8.85% debentures due 2001 ($8,000,000 to be retired annually under sinking fund commencing 1987)	$125,000	$125,000
8⅛% notes due 1986	75,000	75,000
8⅛% debentures due 1996 ($4,000,000 to be retired annually under sinking fund commencing 1982)	53,990	60,000
5% to 8% industrial development and pollution control revenue bonds payable 1985 to 2008	67,950	62,250
9¾% to 13% notes due 1981 to 1985	13,552	31,704
7½% notes due 1997 ($1,625,000 to be retired annually commencing 1983)	25,000	25,000
7.3% to 9.4% notes due 1981 to 1983	8,130	14,746
4½% sinking fund debentures due 1989 ($1,750,000 retired annually under sinking fund)	12,223	12,953
Other notes payable through 1991	10,054	9,215
Total	**$390,899**	**$415,868**

The aggregate maturities and sinking fund requirements (stated in thousands) on long-term debt for the next five years are as follows: 1980, $9,145; 1981, $10,477; 1982, $7,315; 1983, $9,670; and 1984, $11,399.

The Company has revolving credit agreements with groups of major domestic and foreign banks totalling $150,000,000 at December 31, 1979. The domestic agreement provides for borrowings up to $100,000,000 through December 31, 1982, at which time outstanding borrowings may be converted into a four-year term loan. The foreign revolving credit agreement provides for borrowings up to $50,000,000 through March 1, 1984. At December 31, 1979 there were no borrowings under either agreement.

Under the Company's most restrictive debt agreement, approximately $172,000,000 would have been available at December 31, 1979 for dividends and reacquisitions of capital stock.

Stock Option Plans

Options under all plans are granted at the market price of the shares on the dates of the grants. Transactions during 1978 and 1979 for such plans are as follows:

Options outstanding, December 31, 1977 (at per-share prices from $6.59 to $23.72) of which 668,552 shares were exercisable	**1,440,572**
Changes in options during 1978:	
Exercised (at per-share prices from $6.59 to $17.53)	(133,800)
Lapsed or cancelled	(19,760)
Options outstanding, December 31, 1978 (at per-share prices from $6.59 to $23.72) of which 834,412 shares were exercisable	**1,287,012**
Changes in options during 1979:	
Granted	216,400
Exercised (at per-share prices from $6.59 to $17.53)	(129,040)
Lapsed or cancelled	(34,200)
Options outstanding, December 31, 1979 (at per-share prices from $6.59 to $23.72) of which 900,712 shares were exercisable	**1,340,172**

The number of shares available for granting additional options was 892,884 at December 31, 1978 and 700,484 at December 31, 1979.

Pension Plans

The Company has several pension plans covering substantially all employees. The total cost of these plans, including amortization of prior service cost was $14,000,000 for 1979 and $13,800,000 for 1978. The policy of the Company is to fund pension cost accrued. As of December 31, 1979, the actuarially-computed vested benefits were fully funded. Unfunded prior service costs approximated $39,000,000 at December 31, 1979, and are being amortized principally over 40 years from the dates such costs were established.

Exhibit 3.3 *(Continued)*

NOTES TO FINANCIAL STATEMENTS

BUSINESS SEGMENTS

The Company operates in three domestic industries, Agricultural, Chemicals, and Plastics, as well as in the foreign area. The Agricultural Chemicals and Fertilizer and Mining divisions and Seeds compose the Agricultural industry. The Chemicals industry includes the Industrial Chemicals, Specialty Chemicals, Food Ingredients and Chemical Systems divisions. Information concerning the Company's operating industries is shown below:

NET SALES TO UNAFFILIATED CUSTOMERS	1979	1978	1977	1976
		(Dollars in thousands)		
U.S. Group				
Domestic				
Agricultural	$ 352,127	$ 284,469	$ 254,514	$ 223,850
Chemicals	747,034	687,541	648,451	584,376
Plastics	156,236	142,269	152,244	126,980
	1,255,397	**1,114,279**	**1,055,209**	**935,206**
Export				
Agricultural	32,418	22,354	36,510	54,946
Chemicals	65,854	49,640	43,797	37,625
Plastics	4,033	4,112	5,516	9,364
	102,305	**76,106**	**85,823**	**101,935**
Transfers between U.S. Segments — at cost				
Agricultural	9,696	9,012	11,737	11,056
Chemicals	29,995	23,610	23,774	25,304
Eliminations	(39,691)	(32,622)	(35,511)	(36,360)
Transfers to Foreign Group — at market				
Agricultural	6,936	3,556	4,701	5,097
Chemicals	16,262	10,640	8,960	8,786
Plastics	1,443	1,367	1,865	1,750
	24,641	**15,563**	**15,526**	**15,633**
Total U.S. Group Sales				
Agricultural	401,177	319,391	307,462	294,949
Chemicals	859,145	771,431	724,982	656,091
Plastics	161,712	147,748	159,625	138,094
Eliminations	(39,691)	(32,622)	(35,511)	(36,360)
	1,382,343	**1,205,948**	**1,156,558**	**1,052,774**
Foreign Group	**168,458**	**137,729**	**91,728**	**62,859**
Eliminations	(24,641)	(15,563)	(15,526)	(15,633)
Total Net Sales	**$1,526,160**	**$1,328,114**	**$1,232,760**	**$1,100,000**

OPERATING INCOME	1979	1978	1977	1976
U.S. Group				
Agricultural	$ 107,407	$ 89,332	$ 76,474	$ 78,360
Chemicals	160,481	159,717	154,469	145,470
Plastics	(33,081)	4,253	13,096	15,645
	234,807	**253,302**	**244,039**	**239,475**
Foreign Group	**36,714**	**30,638**	**15,910**	**8,345**
Total Operating Income	**271,521**	**283,940**	**259,949**	**247,820**
Interest Expense	(31,839)	(37,923)	(35,198)	(30,968)
Foreign Currency Losses	(3,616)	(5,803)	(6,677)	(4,154)
Interest and Dividend Income	10,227	12,044	10,612	10,458
Corporate Expenses	(50,848)	(51,652)	(42,046)	(40,630)
Other Unallocated (Expense) Income — Net	(9,209)	(10,835)	844	(386)
Earnings before Provision for Income Taxes	**$ 186,236**	**$ 189,771**	**$ 187,484**	**$ 182,140**

Exhibit 3.3 *(Continued)*

DEPRECIATION EXPENSE	1979	1978	1977	1976
		(Dollars in thousands)		
U.S. Group				
Agricultural	$ 21,649	$ 19,040	$ 16,287	$ 14,640
Chemicals	48,843	41,159	33,438	23,543
Plastics	11,442	8,168	7,214	3,863
	81,934	**68,367**	**56,939**	**42,046**
Foreign Group	**6,540**	**5,902**	**3,941**	**693**
Total Identifiable Depreciation Expense	**88,474**	**74,269**	**60,880**	**42,739**
Corporate Assets	4,590	4,071	3,169	2,751
Total Depreciation Expense	**$ 93,064**	**$ 78,340**	**$ 64,049**	**$ 45,490**

CAPITAL EXPENDITURES	1979	1978	1977	1976
U.S. Group				
Agricultural	$ 25,690	$ 21,877	$ 29,632	$ 39,351
Chemicals	153,414	109,309	99,411	71,718
Plastics	25,493	38,489	33,097	26,448
	204,597	**169,675**	**162,140**	**137,517**
Foreign Group	**7,335**	**8,215**	**14,420**	**42,015**
Total Identifiable Capital Expenditures	**211,932**	**177,890**	**176,560**	**179,532**
Corporate Assets	27,371	23,306	16,876	19,243
Total Capital Expenditures	**$ 239,303**	**$ 201,196**	**$ 193,436**	**$ 198,775**

ASSETS	1979	1978	1977	1976
U.S. Group				
Agricultural	$ 430,364	$ 387,997	$ 337,411	$ 329,859
Chemicals	761,939	632,807	528,649	446,587
Plastics	216,515	207,067	159,310	119,749
	1,408,818	**1,227,871**	**1,025,370**	**896,195**
Foreign Group	**197,662**	**177,506**	**152,926**	**108,062**
Eliminations	(29,766)	(22,882)	(22,823)	(18,443)
Total Identifiable Assets	**1,576,714**	**1,382,495**	**1,155,473**	**985,814**
Cash and Marketable Securities	55,903	89,007	96,784	122,448
Investments and Advances — Associated Companies	41,412	40,384	34,348	30,568
Corporate Assets	202,205	155,343	142,939	129,671
Total Assets	**$1,876,234**	**$1,667,229**	**$1,429,544**	**$1,268,501**

Exhibit 3.3 *(Continued)*

NOTES TO FINANCIAL STATEMENTS

Leases

The Company's operations include leases of office and warehouse facilities and transportation, manufacturing, data processing and office equipment. The bulk of the Company's leases are operating leases. Capital leases are not significant. The office and warehouse leases expire over the next 20 years, the transportation and manufacturing equipment leases during the next 25 years and the data processing and office equipment leases over the next 5 years. In most cases, management expects that such leases will be renewed or replaced by other leases.

Approximately one-third of the above leases permit the Company to (a) purchase the property, generally at its fair value at the end of the initial lease term, or (b) renew the lease at various rental value options for periods of 1 to 20 years. Portions of office facilities are sublet under leases expiring during the next 14 years.

Rental expense was $17,100,000 for 1979 and $13,300,000 for 1978, net of sublease revenues of $3,600,000 in both years and transportation equipment mileage credits of $3,700,000 in 1979 and $3,900,000 in 1978. Contingent rental payments, escalation charges and restrictions imposed by lease agreements are not significant. Minimum rental commitments before mileage credits under non-cancellable leases at December 31, 1979 are as follows:

	Real Estate Rentals	Real Estate Subleases	Transportation Equipment	Other	Total
	(Dollars in thousands)				
1980	$ 6,000	$ (3,500)	$ 9,800	$2,600	$14,900
1981	5,500	(3,500)	9,400	2,300	13,700
1982	4,800	(3,400)	8,500	1,600	11,500
1983	4,700	(3,100)	7,500	900	10,000
1984	4,200	(3,000)	6,300	500	8,000
Remainder	27,100	(25,400)	34,600	1,600	37,900
	$52,300	**$(41,900)**	**$76,100**	**$9,500**	**$96,000**

Supplementary Earnings Statement Information

	1979	1978
	(Dollars in thousands)	
Inventories entering into the computation of cost of goods sold:		
Beginning of year	$278,313	$233,699
End of year	$318,743	$278,313
Maintenance and repairs	$ 83,877	$ 73,985
Taxes, other than income taxes:		
Property	$ 12,744	$ 12,462
Payroll	17,945	15,264
Other	3,884	3,192
Total	**$ 34,573**	**$ 30,918**
Interest incurred on long-term debt	$ 34,245	$ 34,421

Commitments

Unexpended appropriations for the construction of additional facilities approximated $129,000,000 at December 31, 1979. Portions of these appropriations are covered by firm commitments.

Replacement Cost Information

Unaudited replacement cost information for the two years ended December 31, 1979 and 1978, is included in the Company's Form 10-K to be filed with the Securities and Exchange Commission.

Exhibit 3.3 *(Continued)*

STATEMENT OF CONSOLIDATED STOCKHOLDERS' EQUITY

Stauffer Chemical Company and Subsidiaries

		1979	1978
		(Dollars in thousands)	
Common Stock	**Balance at Beginning of Year**	**$ 55,757**	**$ 55,649**
	Issuance of Common Shares Under Employee Plans (1979 — 91,157 shares including 11,477 reacquired; 1978 — 117,200 shares including 31,090 reacquired)	99	108
	Balance at End of Year	**$ 55,856**	**$ 55,757**
Other Capital	**Balance at Beginning of Year**	**$ 95,936**	**$ 94,996**
	Issuance of Common Shares Under Employee Plans	767	940
	Balance at End of Year	**$ 96,703**	**$ 95,936**
Retained Earnings	**Balance at Beginning of Year**	**$617,628**	**$534,273**
	Net Earnings	135,961	126,015
	Cash Dividends (Per Share: 1979 — $1.075; 1978 — $.975)	(47,132)	(42,660)
	Balance at End of Year	**$706,457**	**$617,628**
Reacquired Stock	**Balance at Beginning of Year**	**$ (7,984)**	**$ (8,289)**
	Issuance of Common Shares Under Employee Plans	113	305
	Balance at End of Year	**$ (7,871)**	**$ (7,984)**
	Total Stockholders' Equity, December 31	**$851,145**	**$761,337**

See information on page 24 and notes to financial statements on pages 30 through 34.

Exhibit 3.3 *(Continued)*

Exhibit 3.4 Stauffer Chemical Company: Transaction Analysis for 1979

Line		Cash	NWA	Marketable Securities	Property, Plant & Equipment	Investment and Advances
1	31 December 78	$24,996	$412,208	$64,011	$903,246	$40,384
2	Net Sales		+1,526,160			
3	Interest and Dividends	+10,227				
4	Cost of Goods Sold/Depreciation		(1,013,594)		(93,204)	
5	SG & A		(161,866)			
6	Research and Development		(36,963)			
7	Interest		(31,839)			
8	Other income	+3,730				
9	Minority Interest					
10	Provision for Taxes		(23,259)			
11	Associates Earnings					+10,800
12	New Owner's Equity	+979				
13	Pay Minority Dividends	(2,133)				
14	Cash Dividends	(47,132)				
15	New Long-Term Debt	+9,475				
16	Current Portion LTD					
17	Pay Cur. portion LTD	(13,599)				
18	Repay Long-Term Debt	(25,299)				
19	New Short-Term Debt	+60,858				
20	Capital Expenditure	(239,303)			+236,485	
21	Amortize Intangibles		+1,905			
22	Sell Fixed Assets	+6,125			(6,125)	
23	Div. from Associates	+9,772				(9,772)
24	Sell Marketable Securities	+32,820		(32,820)		
25	Net Other Assets Minus Liabilities	(2,912)				
26	Cash from Operations	+196,108	(196,108)			
		24,712	476,644	31,191	1,040,542	41,412

Intangibles	Other	Short-Term Debt	Current Portion of Long-Term Debt	Other Liabilities	Long-Term Debt	Deferred Taxes	Minority Interest	Owner's Equity
$31,273	$50,066	$135,841	$13,599	$31,239	$415,868	$108,289	$60,011	$761,337
								+1,526,160
								+10,227
								(1,106,658)
								(161,866)
								(36,963)
								(31,839)
								+3,730
							+16,555	(16,555)
						+37,816		(61,075)
								+10,800
								+979
							(2,133)	
								(47,132)
					+9,475			
			+9,145		(9,145)			
			(13,599)					
					(25,299)			
		+60,858						
	+2,818							
(1,905)								
	+13,331			+10,419				
29,368	66,215	196,699	9,145	41,658	390,899	146,105	74,433	851,145

with owner's equity on the right. Now work through the available information. Remember that each line of the analysis must balance. Any increase in an asset must be balanced by an equal decrease in another asset or by an increase in a liability or in the owner's equity.

There are several useful rules to remember:

1. If the item might correctly be called nonoperating, or if you are unsure at this point, do not make an entry in the net working assets column. Make an entry instead in the cash column. For example, dividends received by a company are not part of its operating income. They will therefore be an increase to cash and an increase to owner's equity.
2. If you cannot completely understand a transaction while working through the information, leave it until later. By then, you may have more information that relates to it.
3. If there is a conflict of information, especially in relation to the precise numbers involved, between the Statement of Changes in Consolidated Financial Position and the income statement, balance sheet, or the notes to either of these, always prefer the numbers recorded in the latter. Auditing standards are never applied as strictly to the Statement of Changes as to the other statements. In fact, management often presents the Statement of Changes in an unaudited form. (Statement of Changes is sometimes called Funds Flow Statement, or Statement of Changes in Working Capital. There is no strict rule as to its name.)

In performing a transaction analysis, you should follow a set routine for recording information. First work through all the information contained in the income statement (Exhibit 3.2). Then work through the note showing changes in owner's equity (Exhibit 3.3). The owner's equity column should now balance. Now use the Statement of Changes in Consolidated Financial Position (Exhibit 3.3) to help you balance each column, working across from right to left. It will be necessary to make assumptions because companies do not always disclose enough information.

In practice, different analysts make different assumptions. The quality of your cashflow analysis depends on how reasonable your assumptions are. You are encouraged to work through this example on paper.

STEP 1. Enter beginning and ending balances for the year from balance sheet on your work sheet. Check that assets equal liabilities plus owner's equity. (NWA stands for Net Working Assets)

STEP 2. Work through the income statement. Note the following:

Line 3. Interest and Dividends received are nonoperating items for a manufacturing company. They are shown in the cash column. For a complete picture, tax on this income should be calculated, deducted from $10,227, and deducted from $23,259 in line 10.

Line 4. Depreciation of $93,204 was disclosed in a note and is included in the Cost of Goods Sold figure. It is assumed that other assets are not depreciated. (This may be unrealistic, but see line 25.)

Line 7. It is assumed that all interest is cash related. Some interest could be amortization of bond discount but examination of the note on Long-Term Debt suggests not.

Line 8. Other Income is nonoperating income by definition.

Line 9. Minority Interest represents the share of minorities in Stauffer's consolidated income, and therefore, it is a nonoperating and noncash expense.

Line 10. Reference to the note on Income Taxes confirms the split between current and deferred taxes shown in the statement of changes in consolidated financial position.

Line 11. Equity in Earnings of Associates represents the Stauffer Company's share of their profits. It is accordingly a noncash revenue and a nonoperating item. Dividends from Associates appear on line 23.

STEP 3. From the note on Owner's Equity we check the information in the Statement of Changes as to new stock issued (line 12).

STEP 4. Work from the right, using the Statement of Changes and notes to the accounts.

Line 13. Minority Interest could decrease if Stauffer purchased additional shares in those subsidiaries. However, payment of dividends to Minorities seems more probable. Minority Interest now balances.

Line 14. From the Statement of Changes. Owner's Equity now balances.

Line 15. From the Statement of Changes.

Lines 16 and 17. Current Portion of Long-Term Debt by definition is that part due for payment within 12 months.

Line 18. With line 16 equals $34,444—see Statement of Changes. Paying debt decreases cash. Long-Term Debt now balances.

Line 19. By definition, New Short-Term Debt increases cash. The notes confirm that this is new commercial paper. However, as short-term debt is included in working capital, this does not show up on the Statement of Changes as a source of cash, only as net change.

Line 20. Sometimes it is necessary to leave a column until more information is available. Accordingly Other Liabilities and Other Assets for the moment are left on one side. From the Statement of Changes sheet, we know that Property Disposals were $6,125. In this case (and normally), this is net book value, as gains or losses on disposal are included in income according to the company's policies. We also know that Depreciation was $93,204. To balance the Plant, Property, and Equipment column, we need $236,485. Accordingly, of the $239,303 Capital Expenditure shown in the Statement of Changes, $236,485 is assumed to be plant and $2,818 to be an increase in other assets.

Line 21. It is normal to amortize intangibles, so the expense of $1,905 must be already included in Selling, General, and Administrative Expense in line 5. We assumed that all these were cash expenses, but this one is not. It is therefore added back to net working assets since it is a noncash expense and was wrongly included in $161,866 in line 5. No acquisition took place during 1979, so there could not have been an increase in this asset.

Line 22. From the Statement of Changes. As we do not know gain or loss on sales, we can assume cash received was net book value. If the amount of gain or loss was known, an adjustment would be made.

Line 23. See line 11.

Line 24. Marketable securities must have been sold.

Line 25. Only Other Assets and Other Liabilities remain unexplained. Unfortunately, there is nothing here to help us determine the nature of these items. The analyst has accordingly "plugged" the numbers by a net decrease to cash of $2,912. Given more information, this deficiency in the analysis could be remedied. However, it is not likely to affect cash from operations and is not considered material given the cash from operations of $196,108 (line 26). This is a typical example of the need to make assumptions.

We are now ready to construct the sources and uses of cash statement from the cash column of our transaction analysis.

Sources and Uses of Cash
Stauffer Chemical Company, 1979
(in millions of dollars)

Sources		Uses	
Cash from Operations	$196	Capital Expenditure	$239
Other Income	24	Pay Dividends	47
New Equity	1	Pay Minorities	2
New Long-Term Debt	9	Repay Long-Term Debt	39
New Short-Term Debt	61	Purchase Other Assets (Net)	3
Sale of Assets	6		
Sale of Marketable Securities	33		
	330		330

Observations

Funds from operations was $260 million and the increase in net working assets was $64 million, hence cash from operations was $196 million. Net working assets/sales ratio was 31% in 1978 and 31.2% in 1979, indicating a stable situation in regard to terms of trade. After deducting cost of dividends, cash from operations plus other income covered $173 million of the $236 million net new capital investment. Sale of marketable securities of $33 million and net new debt of $31 million made up the shortfall. There was a shift from long- to short-term debt, probably due to a rise in long-term interest rates combined with severe restrictions in long-term debt markets. Note that cash from operations was greater than reported net income of $136 million, mainly because of the size of depreciation and deferred taxes.

SUMMARY

Cash from operations represents the normal source of repayment of debt. It can be calculated from the changes in the net working assets. Nonoperating items and nonrecurring items are carefully excluded so that the cash flow analysis shows sources and uses of cash to enable conclusions to be drawn about the year being examined.

Negative cash from operations is normally a serious indication of financial problems unless accompanied by strong and profitable growth. If more than one out of the three most recent years show negative cash from operations, then this is strong evidence of a deteriorating situation. Further, in a study published in 1968 (see Chapter 8), Beaver found that cashflow/total liabilities was the single most significant ratio in predicting a company's likelihood of future collapse.[1] This was confirmed by another article on cashflow analysis and the final years of the W. T. Grant Company, which showed that negative cashflows were a much better leading indicator of financial weakness than were traditional ratios.[2] Accordingly, positive cash from operations is an important requirement for normal lending.

PROBLEMS

1. Perform a transaction analysis, and obtain a sources and uses of cash for Wonderdrug for 19X0.
2. Why is nonoperating income and expense excluded from cash from operations?

[1]W. H. Beaver, "Financial Ratios as Predictors of Failure," *Journal of Accounting Research*, 4 (1968): Supplement.

[2]James A. Largay and Clyde P. Strickney, "Cash Flows, Ratio Analysis, and the W. T. Grant Bankruptcy," Amos Tuck School of Business Administration, no. 180 (1980).

3. Suppose a company includes in its operating income a gain on a sale of trade investments. Where would this be shown on the transaction analysis sheet?
4. Suppose a company shows a loss on the sale of a subsidiary. You are able to trace the disposal of fixed assets associated with this sale, and also the reduction of long-term debt associated with this sale. What other asset or liability might change as a result of this sale?

4 Corporate Structure

Those who are not lawyers, accountants, or bankers are usually unaware of the complex corporate structure of large businesses. They think of Ford or British Steel as just one big company. If they are a bit better informed, they recognize that the word *group* is frequently used about a business organization. And rightly so, for a business organization is generally a group of separate companies, with a parent company and subsidiaries. This chapter is about the effects of corporate structure on consolidated financial statements. It is also about how bankers decide which member of the group will be the borrower.

First, we will review accounting practice under GAAP as it affects consolidations. A consolidated statement presents the results and balance sheets of a family of companies as if they were the results of one company. Thus, it largely ignores the legal separation of the entities in the group. A consolidated corporation has no legal existence by itself; it is just an accounting convenience. Consider for a moment a company with two subsidiaries. Let's call the parent "DADCO" and the subsidiaries "Charley" and "George." DADCO makes no sales, nor does it purchase goods. Charley and George do all the manufacturing and selling. DADCO performs only one function: It owns all the shares in Charley and George and receives dividends as owner. During a period, Charley sells 15 apples, including 2 to George, and George sells 20 apples. A consolidated sales statement shows that DADCO sold 33 apples, since intercompany transactions are eliminated.

The first point, therefore, is that inclusion of an item in consolidated statements does not by itself reveal which member of the family it relates to. The second point to remember is that transactions within the family do not count. All that consolidated statements show are transactions, with the rest of the world, and assets, and liabilities vis-á-vis the rest of the world.

Analysts usually face problems when dealing with that part of the consolidated balance sheet representing owner's equity, including the ownership of parts of subsidiaries by persons outside the group (minority interests), together with an intangible asset that sometimes arises on consolidation which does not appear in the balance sheet of either the parent or the subsidiary. In consolidations, the owner's equity shown in the consolidated statement is always that of the parent or top company. The reason is simply that a consolidation replaces an investment item with the actual assets and liabilities comprising that investment (that is, its net asset value). This is best illustrated by an example.

Example 4.1. Once more, DADCO owns Charley and George. DADCO has always paid out in cash to its owners all the dividend income which it has received from Charley and George. DADCO has owner's equity of 100, and its investment in George cost 60 and in Charley 40. Thus, DADCO (by itself) shows:

Owner's Equity 100	Investment 100

This is a very simple balance sheet, with assets at cost.[1] Unfortunately, it tells us nothing about the affairs of the group.

Suppose Charley and George have the following balance sheets:

Charley		George	
Assets	300	Assets	500
Liabilities	270	Liabilities	440
Owner's Equity	30	Owner's Equity	60
	300		500

Using the procedure of expanding the investment item by replacing it with the actual assets and liabilities, we now see the consolidation:

DADCO (Consolidated)			
Liabilities	710	Assets	800
Owner's Equity	100	Goodwill	10
	810		810

This assumes there are no intercompany items. "Goodwill" refers to the intangible asset arising on consolidation. Notice that this intangible asset represents the amount by which the cost of Charley (40) exceeded the net assets acquired (which is Charley's owner's equity of 30). Notice also that, if we added Charley and George's equity to that of the parent, we would get a nonsense result. In consolidations, therefore, the investment in the ownership of a subsidiary which would otherwise be shown as investments is replaced by that subsidiary's actual external assets and liabilities. If the recorded cost of the investment is different from the actual net assets, then there will be a gain or loss on consolidation—that is, an asset for the gain and a reserve for the loss.

[1]This would also represent investments on an equity accounting basis if dividends received were always equal to Charley and George's net income.

MINORITY INTERESTS

So far we have dealt with 100% owned subsidiaries. What happens with partially owned subsidiaries? The rule in GAAP is that, if more than 50% is owned, they must be consolidated. Once again, let's look at an example.

Example 4.2. Suppose DADCO buys another subsidiary, Fiona, but is only able to obtain 60% of Fiona's shares. The other 40% remain with Fiona's previous owners. On consolidation, this 40% will become a minority interest, since it represents claims by outsiders on the combined equity of the business. These outsiders will on consolidation appear as if they were external liabilities of the group. Of course, they are not really liabilities, since they do not represent money owned in the way in which debt is owed. If the minority interest is large, it may well cause problems in estimating total owner's equity or tangible net worth, especially when constructing ratios of debt to net worth, such as are used in term loan covenants (see Chapter 9).

Fiona has assets of 200 and liabilities of 130, with owner's equity of 70. DADCO's consolidated statements—after it raised 42 in new cash from its own investors to enable it to buy 60% of Fiona for exactly 60% of 70 (that is, 42)—will now be:

Liabilities	840	Assets	1,000
Minority Interest	28	Goodwill	10
Owner's Equity	142		
	1,010		1,010

Notice that goodwill did not change, because 60% of Fiona was acquired for exactly the net asset value.

It will be useful at this point to list ways in which minority interest will change from year to year, since this often will require explanation by analysts. Minority interest increases when the following occurs:

1. Profits earned by a partially owned subsidiary must be shared between the parent and the minority interest. Hence, if Fiona's net income is 200, minority interest will increase by 40% of 200 (80), while owner's equity increases by the rest.
2. If the parent sells some of its shares in a partially owned subsidiary to outsiders. But if the parent reduces its ownership to less than 50%, the subsidiary will become an associated company, and thus there will then be no minority interest.
3. If the subsidiary raises new shares from its owners either in proportions equal to their ownership or even disproportionately.
4. When fixed assets are revalued, resulting in a gain to reserves (owner's equity). Such revaluation is allowed in some countries, though not the United States.

Decreases in minority interest will occur in the following instances:

1. As a result of losses occurring in that subsidiary.
2. As a result of dividends paid to the outside owners. But only if these dividends exceed the outside owners' share of that year's earnings will minority interest decrease at the end of the period because of dividend payments alone.
3. When a subsidiary is sold completely.
4. When a subsidiary becomes an associated company. That is, if a parent sells shares in a subsidiary to such an extent that its ownership falls below 50%, then the parent will not consolidate the subsidiary's figures. Hence, on the consolidated balance sheet, minority interest will decrease, or disappear altogether, if this was the only partially owned subsidiary.

SUBSIDIARIES NOT CONSOLIDATED

It is quite possible for a company to have subsidiaries which are not included in consolidated balance sheets or in consolidated income statements. To be precise, such subsidiaries are not excluded entirely from such figures; they are treated as investments, even though the parent owns 51% or more. In the United States, accounting principles permit companies not to consolidate subsidiaries if the inclusion of such subsidiaries would not present a clear picture:

> Separate statements for a subsidiary or group of subsidiaries would be preferable if the presentation of financial information would be more informative than would the inclusion of such subsidiaries in the consolidation. For example separate statements may be required for a subsidiary which is a bank or insurance company, and may be preferable for a finance company where the parent and other subsidiaries are engaged in manufacturing operations.[2]

In the United Kingdom, the rule is similar.

In other countries, there is wider variation. In Italy, until recently, consolidated statements were not produced at all. In Germany it is still the practice to exclude foreign subsidiaries from the consolidation, irrespective of the size of the subsidiary. This is a convenient practice for very large companies in that often a financing subsidiary can be created to raise funds for the group as a whole; if it is not consolidated, these financial obligations are not shown on the consolidated balance sheet.

As an analyst, you must decide in each case whether nonconsolidated subsidiaries should be added to the consolidation. For instance, if a total liabilities/tangible net worth figure is being constructed, there seems little sense in not including such finance company liabilities because they certainly

[2] *Handbook of Accounting Standards*. Published annually by the American Institute of Certified Public Accountants. Taken from Volume III, paragraph 2051.04.

represent claims of outsiders on the business that will have to be satisfied from group cashflow. On the other hand, if the subsidiary is a bank or insurance company that is not related to the parent company and that stands by itself for financing purposes, there may be good reason not to include the subsidiary's liabilities in the calculation. Thus, consideration of the purpose of the ratio and the nature of the subsidiary helps to determine whether to include these figures or not.

DEBT PRIORITY

If asked whether it is better to lend to a parent company or to a subsidiary, most people, I suspect, would answer "the parent"—and in most cases, they would be wrong. This is because of the priority of creditors in bankruptcy laws. Such laws, of course, vary in detail from country to country, but they always place shareholders at the bottom of the list of those with claims against the company.

Let's consider an example. Anyone lending to DADCO, our parent or holding company earlier in this chapter, should know that its assets consist only of shares in Charley, George, and Fiona, its three subsidiaries. Because DADCO is a pure holding company, it does not have operating assets of its own. If DADCO cannot pay, its lenders may take possession of its assets. However, in so doing, the lenders become stockholders in Charley, George, and Fiona. In this way, their claims on the assets—the true operating assets of the group—are inferior to those of creditors and holders of preferred stock in the subsidiaries. It follows, therefore, that in general lenders to the subsidiaries are ahead of lenders to the parent in terms of what is known as "debt priority." This will be illustrated by a more detailed case, which will also demonstrate the need for consolidating statements. Note carefully that a *Consolidating* statement shows each company's figures and how they are added together to make the *Consolidated* statement.

Example 4.3. Bovington Holdings, Inc., owns one subsidiary, Bovington Books. In 19X0 a bank makes a $150,000 three-year term loan to Bovington Holdings on the basis of the following consolidated balance sheet and cashflow statement:

Bovington Holdings, Inc.
Consolidated Balance Sheet, December 31, 19X9

Cash	$ 80	Short-Term Debt	$ 100
Accounts Receivable	150	Accounts Payable	100
Inventory	250	Long-Term Debt	500
Plant (Net)	820	Deferred Tax	75
	1,300	Owner's Equity	525
	$1,300		$1,300

Cashflow Statement

Year to	December, 19X9 (Actual)	19X0 (Projected)	19X1 (Projected)	19X2 (Projected)
Funds from operations	$260	$ 280	$ 310	$ 330
Less increase in net working assets	(80)	(90)	(100)	(100)
Cash from operations	180	190	210	230
Plant purchases	(60)	(240)	(90)	(90)
Repay long-term debt	(70)	(120)	(120)	(120)
New loan	—	150	—	—
Increase in cash	50	(20)	0	20
Ending cash balance	80	60	60	80

As can be seen, the purpose of the loan is to buy a new plant, and repayment will come out of cashflow over three years. Unfortunately, by the end of the first six months, the company had suffered a downturn in demand and is unable to make its first repayment of $25,000. This is what its consolidated balance sheet shows:

Cash	$ 100	Short-Term Debt	$ 100
Accounts Receivable	150	Accounts Payable	100
Inventory	278	Long-Term Debt	650
Plant (Net)	960	Deferred Tax	93
		Owner's Equity	545
	1,488		1,488

Net income of 20 has been earned: Adding back depreciation of 50 and the deferred tax charge of 18, funds from operations is 88; and as net working assets have only increased by 28, cash from operations is 60. Why can't Bovington pay? The answer lies in the consolidating statements:

Bovington Holdings
(Company alone)

Cash	$ 10	Short-Term Debt	100
Equity in Subsidiaries	750	Long-Term Debt	150
Other Assets	10	Equity	520
	770		770

Bovington Books

Cash	$ 90	Accounts Payable	100
Accounts Receivable	150	Long-Term Debt	500
Inventory	278	Deferred Tax	93
Plant (Net)	950	Owner's Equity	775
	1,468		1,468

Bovington Books has the cash alright, but it cannot pay its parent because of restrictions in its own existing long-term debt agreement that limit its payment of dividends, management fees, and loans to the parent. If it could "upstream" the money—that is, pay some more to the parent—there would not be a problem. What happened was that the parent "downstreamed" the money to Bovington Books and now cannot get it back. If the bank lends money to the parent, it will be in no better position, since the lenders to Bovington Books have debt priority.

In this instance, a better route would have been to lend to Bovington Books directly, thus getting nearer to the cashflow, or to have taken a guarantee from Bovington Books for the benefit of the holding Company loan. This would have given the lender a direct claim on the subsidiary's assets.

Moral: Always lend as near as possible to the source of the cashflow from operations on which you have chosen to rely for payment.

Example 4.4. Sometimes a parent company also has operating assets of its own. In that case, loans can safely be made up to some level which will be covered by the parents short-term operating assets. One way of presenting this is to specify that all the parent's ownership of long-term assets, including investments in subsidiaries, must be covered by long-term sources of funds.

Intercon shows the following figures for the parent company alone:

Cash	$ 170	Accounts Payable	$ 300
Inventories	382	Short-Term Debt	650
Receivables	529	Accrued Taxes	420
Plant (Net)	1,423	Long-Term Debt	4,333
Investments in Subsidiaries	7,106	Owner's Equity	3,907
	9,610		9,610

Applying the rule suggested, Plant plus Investment (1,423 + 7,106 = 8,529) must be covered by Long-term Debt and owner's Equity (4,333 + 3,907 = 8,240). Thus, in this case, there is no room for additional Short-Term Debt without breaking the rule.

MORE ON CONSOLIDATING STATEMENTS

As we saw in Example 4.3, consolidating statements comprise a set of figures for each member of a group. They enable you to review the financial condition and operating ability of each member, whether subsidiary or parent. You can then separate weak companies from strong: those that have too little capital, those with the heaviest debt, those with weak sales, and those with heavy expenses. You may find that one or more of the subsidiaries is a regular loss maker. Another one could be the "cash cow" of the whole group, which if it were sold, would adversely affect the other members. You can determine the individual capital base of each corporation, whether or not there are preferred stock issues made by subsidiaries, and the extent of intercompany support.

ORGANIZATION CHARTS

Where a group is particularly complex, it will help to produce a chart of corporate relationships. A chart of this kind for the Thomson Brandt Group of France as of 1981 is shown as Exhibit 4.1. All companies whose figures are part of the consolidated balance sheet and profit and loss are shown, with their shareholdings in each other set out as of the date of the chart. Thomson Brandt is one of Europe's largest companies and also has one of the most complicated corporate structures. The chart helps to show who owns whom.

DEBT PRIORITY SCHEDULE

Once you decide to which company your bank is going to lend, a debt priority schedule can be drawn up. This will show how much debt is senior to yours in terms of priority. You will want to know whether the debt is secured or unsecured and whether it is short or long term. First, however, let's review the normal priority of claims on a company's assets. These claims arise when a company is in liquidation and are established by law. In most countries, the order in which claims are settled is the same: First are the preferred creditors; second, the secured creditors; third, the unsecured creditors; and finally, the shareholders.

Included in the preferred creditors group are government agencies with any claims for taxes, social security payments, and so on. These are generally given first priority. After all, governments make the rules in bankruptcy, so they have an advantage over all other kinds of creditors. Next, the employees usually have a limited amount of claims of wages, and there are other preferred claims, such as the liquidation expenses.

Exhibit 4.2 Debt Priority Schedule, Low Leverage (in millions of pounds)

	Long-Term	Short-Term	Total
Parent Company			
Unsecured	£10.0	£ 0.8	£10.8
Secured*	0.4	—	0.4
Subsidiaries			
Secured*	6.2	4.0	10.2
Unsecured*	2.5	36.0	38.5
	19.1	40.8	59.9

Percentage secured	17.6%
*Prior debt	£49.1 million
Tangible net worth	£420 million
Prior debt/tangible net worth	12%

Since secured creditors have assets to realize which may cover their portion of the debt, unsecured creditors—in which category banks often find themselves—are those with the least chance of full repayment in the event of corporate collapse. Shareholders, being by definition equity risk takers, are paid with anything left after all other claims, including preferred stock, are settled.

Two interesting examples are shown based on two British companies' figures as they were at the end of 1978. In both cases, a bank was considering lending unsecured to the parent company. Prior debt would thus be all secured loans to the parent and all loans (unsecured and secured) to the subsidiaries.

Exhibit 4.3 Debt Priority Schedule, High Leverage (in millions of pounds)

	Long-Term	Short-Term	Total
Parent Company			
Unsecured	£ 69.9	£ 1.1	£ 71.0
Secured*	—	—	—
Subsidiaries			
Unsecured*	68.7	19.3	88.0
Secured*	4.0	0.9	4.9
	142.6	21.3	163.9

Percentage secured	2.9%
*Prior debt	£92.9 million
Tangible net worth	£152.3 million
Prior debt/tangible net worth	61%

Exhibit 4.2 shows a company with very little total debt in relation to tangible net worth; Exhibit 4.3 shows a highly leveraged situation. In Exhibit 4.2, 82% of the debt is ahead of (prior to) the bank's proposed loan to the parent company, whereas in Exhibit 4.3, only 57% is ahead of the bank. It might seem, therefore, that Exhibit 4.3 is more attractive simply on the basis of debt priority. But that would be wrong, since a credit decision must consider not only debt priority but also total leverage, stability of cashflow and many other factors. Notice, for instance, the size of total debt/tangible net worth in Exhibit 4.3 compared with Exhibit 4.2. In the former, debt is 61% of tangible net worth, whereas in the latter, it is only 14.3%. As it happens, Exhibit 4.2 is Thorn Electrical Industries, and Exhibit 4.3 is EMI, which Thorn subsequently acquired by takeover.

PARENT SUPPORT FOR SUBSIDIARIES

In a book on credit analysis, it is important to review the extent to which parent companies support their subsidiaries. Support is sometimes by guarantee and sometimes by what are known as "comfort letters." Another form of parent support can be obtained when a bank requires that parent company loans be subordinated to the bank's own loans and not be repaid before the bank is paid in full. Sometimes the support is not apparent and may in fact not exist.

Comfort letters are frequently used in international situations. Although it is rare for companies with international business to walk away from their subsidiaries in foreign countries, this has happened on one or two unusual occasions.

Banks are often asked to accept something less than legal guarantees for a variety of reasons. Since guarantees are legal instruments and subject to different rules in different countries, it is not appropriate to discuss these rules here. However, in view of the fact that comfort letters are moral obligations (only in very rare cases do they represent legally binding contractual obligations), it seems sensible to consider the extent to which such letters strengthen the case for lending to a subsidiary.

The general principle to bear in mind is that a comfort letter is not a guarantee of payment. If you went into a court of law with such a letter, there would be one very solid reason why the document would be rejected as a basis on which you could claim repayment. This reason is that there is a long established, universally applied principle of law that requires courts to determine what was in the minds of the respective parties to an agreement based on what a reasonable observer would conclude. It is immediately obvious that if a guarantee of payment had been intended by the parent, it would have used a specified form of words, perhaps even a standard bank form, guaranteeing payment. By their very existence, comfort letters are recognized as a different type of arrangement from guarantees. Further, in

English law, for instance, for a binding contract to exist, there must be an intention to create legal relationships between the two parties. This would be hard to prove if the parent argued that the reason it did not issue a guarantee was that it had no such intention, and at the same time it showed that there was a legal contract between the bank and its subsidiary to which it was an uninvolved third party.

Comfort letters should be analyzed in four ways: the reason for the absence of a guarantee, the borrower's own condition, the parent company's relationship to the borrower, and the actual text of the comfort letter. The most common reason for issuing a comfort letter is that competitive pressure among banks permits the parent to use its financial strength to avoid issuing a guarantee. Ever since banks have expanded overseas in search of opportunities with the overseas operations of their multinational customers, the prevalence of comfort letters has increased. Remember that the home country bank in a foreign country dealing with the subsidiary there of one of its large domestic customers is able to take comfort from the fact that it has substantial muscle to apply to the parent at home should there ever be a problem in the overseas branch. Other reasons for issuing comfort letters may be that the parent has a worldwide policy of issuing no guarantees or that it is restricted from doing so by prior existing loan agreements or indentures. Or there could be a tax reason: A guarantee could result in an assumption of what is called "constructive dividends" from the subsidiary. That is to say, there would sometimes be payments from the subsidiary which would be taxed as dividends (even though they were not) if the parent guaranteed the debts of the subsidiary. Another reason might be that the parent would have to obtain exchange control permission in its home country to issue the guarantee but not the comfort letter. Finally, if the parent's loan agreements already contain clauses specifying that a default by any subsidiary is treated as a default by the parent, the presence of a guarantee may be unnecessary if the lender believes in the parent's intention to be financially responsible and to avoid default (and hence renegotiation) of any of its medium-term obligations.

Now as to the borrower's own condition, you should consider the extent to which it is financially able to stand on its own. There is a world of difference between a subsidiary that is in a self-contained marketing situation—not reliant on its parent, neither selling to it, nor buying from it, and probably not having any part of its parent's name as its own name—and the sort of subsidiary which is typically found with weak financial condition, heavily dependent on parent supplies or purchases, and subject to the effects of inter company transfer pricing. The former is probably financially self-supporting, and comfort letters will not even be offered, whereas the latter is completely subject to the will of its parent and requires a strong comfort letter at the very least.

Another point to consider is the degree of economic integration between parent and subsidiary. As a general principle, the more closely the subsidiary is economically integrated, the more reason the parent has to support it.

Perhaps it is an important supplier of parts, or perhaps it represents a key marketing company. In general, you should beware of companies that have no economic importance to the parent, even if they are well integrated with it. Pure sales subsidiaries with no manufacturing capability would be poor credit risks if unsupported by the parent at least by a comfort letter specifying a promise to maintain 100% ownership during the life of the credit facility.

Third, the nature of the parent company's relationship with your bank will need to be analyzed. If as already stated you have substantial influence with the parent, you will be able to exercise much more moral suasion than if this proposed lending relationship with the subsidiary is your only point of contact with the entire group. You should also analyze the parent company's financial condition and watch out for any obstacles to its ability to make good on its moral obligation. These obstacles could include tax problems, exchange control restriction, possible stockholder legal action, or legal restriction in senior debt indentures.

Finally, examine the text of the comfort letter itself. In Exhibit 4.4, we see a very weak form. It contains no promises other than the promise to advise the bank of a change of ownership and really provides extraordinarily little comfort to a lender. On the other hand, Exhibit 4.5 has some statements on which you could rely with reasonable assurance.

The words of this letter quite clearly indicate what the parent will do, short of guaranteeing payment, to ensure that the loan is repaid. Be sure to consider the person signing the letter. What is his or her official rank? The higher the rank, the more you can rely on the letter. Consider also that the

Exhibit 4.4 Weak Comfort Letter

Gentlemen:

As previously discussed with you by representatives of the Treasurer's office of LK Industries, Inc. (the "Company"), the Company has caused a wholly owned subsidiary, LK Canada Ltd. to be incorporated on October 15, 19X1. LK Canada is intended to serve the Company's financing, currency transactions, and cash management requirements in Canada, where the Company has a number of operating subsidiaries. It is the Company's intention to maintain its 100% ownership of LK Canada Ltd., unless the Company notifies you to the contrary.

As discussed with you, the Company requests that the credit facility previously made available by you to LK Systems Canada Limited, an operating subsidiary of the Company, in an amount not to exceed 5,000,000 Canadian Dollars, be made available to LK Canada Ltd. on or after November 2, 19X1. This facility may be increased from time to time but in no event should exceed 25,000,000 Canadian Dollars unless otherwise notified by the Treasurer of this Company.

Please let us know should you have any questions in connection with this matter.

Very truly yours,

LK Industries, Inc.

Exhibit 4.5 Strong Comfort Letter

Gentlemen:

We are writing to acknowledge the credit facility of 10 million Canadian dollars that you have offered to extend to our wholly owned subsidiary LK Canada Ltd. We appreciate your willingness to lend and we are aware of the terms of the facility which have been agreed.

It is our intention to continue our interest in LK Canada Ltd. and we will not reduce our ownership in this company while any part of the debt is outstanding to you, or any contingent liability.

Further, we wish to advise you that it is a matter of policy that LK Industries, Inc. will manage its subsidiaries in such a way that they are able to meet their obligations. We will not permit LK Canada Ltd. to pay any dividends as long as any debt of that company is outstanding to you. Further, we will not guarantee any indebtedness of the borrower without first guaranteeing the indebtedness of the borrower to your bank on an equal basis. The individual whose signature appears below is duly authorized to sign such a letter on behalf of LK Industries, Inc.

Very truly yours,

Treasurer

presence of such a letter at least constitutes a strong argument that the subsidiary was within its authority in negotiating the loan. You should always be concerned that due authority has been granted for such agreements at both subsidiary and parent level.

Two famous examples illustrate better than general discussion the problem of moral support. It should be pointed out that we have no knowledge as to the extent of any oral backing for the lenders in either case. In the first case, in 1960 Freeport Sulphur had a wholly owned subsidiary, Cuban American Nickel Company, operating in Cuba. The subsidiary was autonomous to the extent that it arranged its own financing, without any formal backing from the parent. It appears, however, that the lenders were relying on the strength of the parent when making their loans, since there were over $93 million in liabilities and only $11 million of equity owned by Freeport, which also held nearly $5 million of subordinated notes. When the subsidiary was confiscated by the Castro government in 1960, the lenders were left with their claims but no assets on which to claim other than those of the parent. After due consideration, the board of directors of Freeport concluded that it was their best business judgment not to rescue the lenders because there were no benefits to accrue to Freeport by so doing. Further, any money paid out would have created no benefit to the parent company's stockholders and would not have been tax deductible.

By contrast, the American Express Company, in another case in the 1960s—the "Great Salad Oil Scandal"—concluded that it was in the best interests of the parent to make up some of the losses incurred by creditors of its warehousing subsidiary. It is not necessary to go into the many legal points affecting their decision; however, factors strongly influencing the board were the worldwide reputation of American Express, which would have otherwise been severely weakened, as well as a favorable tax ruling on whether these amounts were tax deductible.

To sum up, then, on parent support for subsidiaries, you must be sure that all the facts of each case are separately and properly reviewed. While comfort letters are widely used, they are of limited value; for instance, they do not generally cover political intervention or fraudulent mismanagement. You should always consider the exact words used, and the extent to which the subsidiary's credit rating can stand alone. And always consider what would happen if the subsidiary were sold without consulting any of the lenders.

PROBLEMS

1. Why is it important to distinguish carefully between an individual statement and a consolidated statement?
2. What is a direct subsidiary? An indirect subsidiary?
3. Under what conditions of ownership is it usually considered proper to consolidate? Discuss.
4. Explain the meaning and significance of a minority interest in a consolidated balance sheet.
5. Briefly explain the elimination of intercompany profits (1) on intercompany inventories and (2) on intercompany sales of fixed assets.
6. Why might the individual statement of a corporation that is one of a related group of corporations be less reliable and significant than a properly prepared consolidated statement of the group as a whole?
7. Why is it usually desirable to obtain and analyze the individual statements of associates?
8. What considerations should be borne in mind in lending to a holding company?
9. In lending to a subsidiary company, why is a consolidated statement still of interest to the analyst?
10. What arrangements may be made to strengthen a loan to a subsidiary company when part of its financing requirements are supplied by the parent company?
11. Explain fully what is meant by the priority of subsidiary debt as to subsidiary assets.

5 Using Financial Ratios

If you can't make 10% on your money, drink it.
BERNARD M. BARUCH

A ratio compares one thing to another. There are so many lessons to be derived from the apocryphal remark attributed to the famous financier Bernard M. Baruch that it probably deserves a chapter of its own. For the moment, however, this chapter is intended to set out how to use financial ratios for credit analysis. We leave aside the questions of the modern approach to portfolio investment. What Baruch is saying, is that a ratio will tell you not only about profitability but also about whether the effort of an investment is worthwhile. In doing so, he stresses the need for comparison. He could have said, "If you don't make $20,000 a year out of the stock market, forget it." But would Baruch have conveyed his message correctly to a very rich person with millions of dollars to invest for whom $20,000 might be a lower return than leaving his or her money in the bank? By using a ratio, he has, of course, made his point with general application to any individual situation.

Many people have annual medical checkups. At that time their heart, lungs, eyesight, weight, blood pressure, and so on are extensively tested. Some items of data are meaningful by themselves (temperature 98.6°); others, however, are not. For instance, it would be of little value to a doctor to know that a man's weight had increased 20 pounds in twelve months without knowing the actual weight at the start of the period. Similarly, it would generally be of little help to know that a man's weight was 200 pounds without knowing his height and his age. Ratios solve the problem.

Analysts perform something like an annual health checkup on a company when they receive its financial statements. Indeed, it is commonplace to speak of a company's financial health. We also hear references to companies as "the ailing giant of the industry" or perhaps as "the vigorous newcomer to the market." This chapter will outline which ratios may be generally useful for determining financial health without attempting to cover all the possible ratios that could be calculated. Chapter 8 presents a model using financial ratios to predict corporate bankruptcy, together with a review of some other research on the use of ratios. Remember, however, that ratios are only as valid as the numbers on which they are based. Financial ratios are based on audited financial statements (see Chapter 2), and those statements may be unrepresentative of the company's condition at dates other than those of the balance sheet. Window dressing is, regrettably, practiced in December by firms who have no connection with businesses seeking bigger sales at Christmas.

Before using ratios, you should be quite sure of what you are looking for. It is a common weakness in teaching financial analysis to overburden the student with ratios without discussing their purpose. Let's therefore state plainly that a lending banker is looking for answers to the following questions:

1. What is the nature of the industry of the borrower? For example, is this a high risk/high return industry? A stable industry? Or is this industry "dying"?
2. How does the borrower compare with its competitors in terms of profits? In terms of sales? In terms of cost structure? In using assets?
3. What is the borrower's financial condition? What expectations can be made regarding cashflows? How high are the obligations of the firm in relation to its size? Is it solvent?

TYPES OF RATIOS

There are four types of financial ratios:

1. *Profitability Ratios.* These are intended to measure the company's ability to earn profits. Since the term *profitability* may reflect different things to different users of financial ratios, no one indicator is presented here as the sole ratio to be used.
2. *Leverage Ratios.* A company uses debt of various types as well as shareholders' funds. The relative use of these two forms will depend on the company's attitude to risk and return. The most popular, although not necessarily the most perfect ratio, is debt/equity.
3. *Liquidity Ratios (Solvency Ratios).* These ratios are intended to measure the ability of one firm to meet its short-term financial obligations without having to liquidate its long-term assets. Chief among these is the current ratio.
4. *Performance Ratios.* These ratios examine the revenues and expenses of the firm, either to look at cost structure or to relate sales performance to the amount of assets used in creating sales. Generally these ratios concentrate on the efficiency with which assets are used.

Exhibit 5.1 lists some selected financial ratios.

Exhibit 5.1 Selected Financial Ratios

Profitability	
Net income/owner's equity	(Return on equity)
Net income/total assets	(Return on assets)
Earnings before interest and taxes/total assets	(Operating efficiency)
Gross profit/total sales	(Gross margin)
Net income/total sales	(Net margin)
Operating income/operating assets	(Excludes investments)
Sales/total assets	
Leverage	
Total liabilities/owner's equity	(Debt/net worth)
Total liabilities/tangible net worth	
Total liabilities/funds from operations	(Debt/cashflow)
Long-term debt/long-term debt plus owner's equity	
Earnings before interest and taxes/interest expense	(Debt service coverage ratio)
Liquidity	
Working capital/total assets	
Working capital/current assets	
Current assets/current liabilities	(Current ratio)
Net working assets/sales	
Cash, marketable securities and receivables/current liabilities	(Quick ratio)

WHY PROFITABILITY?

You may well ask why should a credit analyst be concerned with profitability when cashflow is more important for repayment of loans and less subject to management manipulation through the use of accounting policies. Consider the problem that exists, for instance, when assets are revalued (assuming the national accounting policies permit this). Immediately, owner's equity is increased by the amount of the revaluation (net of any deferred taxes), and since there is no change in revenues minus expenses, one profitability ratio (namely, return on equity) is decreased. What sense does it make to use such a ratio with such an obvious flaw? The answer must be that the analyst does not simply use one ratio for profitability and that if there are obvious distortions, they should be eliminated.

More importantly, profitability in some form is still used by investors in judging whether to provide new equity capital to a firm. It is also used by competitors looking for an attractive new market sector to penetrate either by direct assault or by acquisition. Management will, once it is attracted to a new business sector, be accustomed to making capital investment decisions using measures that are different from those used by external analysts and unavailable to them (net present value, for instance, which in itself measures profitability in relation to cost of capital and partly in relation to size of capital). Thus, there are two reasons why analysts should identify these attractive sectors. The first reason is to assess why they are so profitable, and the second is to see if there are sufficient barriers to entry to protect existing firms. On the other hand, very low profitability will tend to make investors reluctant to invest either in existing or in new companies. The result will be a shortage of capital. Given that low profitability leads to a low rate of profits being retained in the firm, the first consequence will be an increase in the amount of debt used to finance asset increases. With such asset increases in monetary terms being practically inevitable today because of the effects of inflation, it will not be long before the company runs out of debt capacity. There typically follows a period of decline brought about by capital shortage, ultimately leading to collapse. Reasons for corporate collapse and the use of financial ratios in predicting this are covered separately in Chapter 8.

It is my firm belief that there is a certain Darwinian process going on in the business world, as in the natural world, that the "fittest" companies survive, while the less fit ones die. Those that do not survive include those that *will* not respond adequately to change, as well as those that cannot. Profitability is a powerful indicator of fitness, indeed probably the best long-run indicator of corporate health. Some of the measures of profitability are discussed in the following sections.

Return on Equity

The traditional measure of profitability has been return on equity, defined as net income after taxes divided by total shareholders' funds. Investors expect to receive dividends and increases in dividends. Companies have to provide these out of net income and at the same time retain enough profits to permit the business assets to grow, or be replaced, which, given inflation, will mean growth in money terms.

There has been much debate in the corporate finance textbooks over the cost of capital to a firm. Some of this discussion—for instance, the intellectually elegant theories of Modigliani and Miller—has no practical application for the credit analyst, since markets are generally imperfect and investors do not leverage themselves to the extent that the theory requires.

Taking a step-by-step approach will be the best way to try and find what return on equity is actually required at any moment. This approach can be applied in any country where long-term government bonds are sold in an open market and where a premium for risk can be estimated.

The important first step is to recognize that the rate of return on equity which investors as a whole expect to receive must be the same as the cost of equity capital to corporations. Because dividends are normally taxed at different rates in different countries, the pretax return to investors must be considered. Since investors as a group receive only dividends on their shares, their return must be in the form of dividends and growth of dividends. When an individual investor sells to another investor in the market, the sale price represents the purchaser's evaluation of future dividends (discounted at some interest rate which will vary with perceived riskiness), and so the seller is simply realizing in cash his right to receive the dividends. Investor hopes to receive a capital gain—the typical investor sees his income as capital gains and dividends—but of course the company pays out only dividends.

The yield on a share is the dividend divided by the market price. It is not difficult to show that, if dividends must grow at a rate of $g\%$ to provide a return of $k\%$ to the investor, then

$$k = \frac{D_0}{P_0} + g$$

where D_0 is today's dividend and P_0 is today's share price. In other words, the total yield must be the current dividend yield plus the growth in dividends.

The next step is to recognize that, in order to provide dividend growth at a specified rate, the company must earn that overall rate k on its owner's equity, and profit will then grow at that rate g to enable dividends to grow at rate g.

Example 5.1. Wonderdrug's dividend yield is 5%. Suppose that investors expect a total pretax return of 12% for this type of company, then dividends should grow at 7% to give them this. Suppose the company's net income and owner's equity position at the start of a five-year period is set at 12 and 100, respectively. Half of net income is paid out in dividends. (Note that average equity is used, not ending period equity.)

The progression will have to be as follows:

	19X1	19X2	19X3	19X4	19X5
Dividends	6	6.42	6.87	7.35	7.86
Net Income	12	12.84	13.74	14.70	15.72
Average equity	100	107	114.49	122.50	131.07
Required return on equity	12%	12%	12%	12%	12%

Assume that equity in 19X1 is exactly at net book value. Then note that if dividends grow at 7% and other factors remain unchanged, the share price will naturally adjust so that it still shows a 6% dividend yield in 19X2. Hence, the share price will have also grown 5% per annum to 107. It is not difficult to reconcile this with the requirement for capital growth. (Readers can verify the figures in the table by calculation.)

The next step is to recognize that equities are more risky than bonds, and therefore investors require a higher return. Taking long-term government bonds to be a good case of risk-free investment, we then have to ask what premium a balanced diversified equity portfolio should provide over and above the yield for government bonds to compensate for increased risk. The final step will be to require a higher premium from a more volatile or risky company and a lower premium from a more stable company.

Example 5.2. The Geraldine Corporation is believed to be a balanced diversified U.S. corporation whose share price moves very closely in line with stock market averages (that is, a beta of one). If U.S. Government bonds yield 10% and the equity risk premium is 4%, then Geraldine's cost of equity should be 14%.

The question generally arises as to what is a reasonable historic return on equity. Some statistics for U.S. industrial sectors are shown in Table 5.1. I suggest that you develop your own table for the industries and countries in which you are interested. These ratios, however, will be useful only for publicly owned companies, where accounting principles are relatively strict.

It follows from the above discussion that, if business cannot consistently earn a rate equal to what investors require by way of dividends and dividend growth, or if the risk-free rate rises to exceptional levels, business will starve for lack of capital (the risk-free alternatives proving too attractive). It is also alarming to reflect that, in figures collected in 1978 by *Management Today,* a leading British business magazine, the largest 200 companies in the United Kingdom (measured by market capitalization) achieved the following return on equity during 1975–1977, a period of 12–20% inflation:

1975	1976	1977
9.1%	11.2%	11.6%

During this period, the long-term rate of interest averaged 13.5%. Readers are left to themselves to wonder how long it would be (if such conditions persisted) before share prices reflected the fact that investment by companies in capital assets produced lower returns than risk free investment in government securities. A final thought: Bernard Baruch's own 10% figure was struck during a time of negligible inflation. What would he want today?

Earnings before Interest and Taxes/Total Assets

Another vitally important profitability ratio is earnings before interest and taxes/total assets. This is usually shortened to EBIT/TA. It represents what the fundamental operations of the business earned as a return on capital invested before any payment for use of that capital either in dividends or in interest. It is also more useful than return on equity in some ways, since it is calculated before the impact of taxation. Because taxes can be varied by government action and by corporate tax-reduction schemes to exploit tax

	1975	1976	1977	1978	1979	1980	1981	Average for 1975–1981
Broadcasting and movies	19.4	21.0	22.2	21.6	22.2	18.0	N/A	20.73
Mining, crude oil	16.3	16.5	12.3	10.1	16.7	21.0	17.6	15.78
Soap, cosmetics	15.6	16.3	16.5	16.7	17.4	16.9	15.8	16.45
Pharmaceuticals	16.2	15.8	16.7	17.6	18.0	17.9	18.0	17.17
Tobacco	13.5	15.5	15.3	15.8	18.4	19.8	19.5	16.82
Beverages	14.2	15.4	12.2	10.5	15.7	15.6	19.2	14.68
Publishing, printing	11.2	14.7	14.8	15.8	17.9	15.9	16.4	15.24
Aerospace	11.9	14.6	14.4	15.6	19.2	16.2	15.0	15.27
Electronics, appliances	11.2	14.1	15.2	14.9	16.3	16.2	14.3	14.60
Chemicals	12.6	14.1	13.0	13.1	15.2	13.9	13.5	13.62
Shipbuilding and transporation equipment	10.8	13.9	15.4	15.9	18.1	14.4	14.4	14.70
Metal products	13.1	13.8	13.9	15.3	16.0	15.3	14.1	14.50
Motor vehicles	5.8	13.8	14.8	15.4	15.7	8.1	7.6	11.60
Industrial and farm equipment	11.9	13.4	13.7	15.2	15.4	13.3	13.9	13.82
Petroleum refining	11.9	13.0	13.1	13.4	19.1	19.4	16.4	15.18
Paper, fiber, and wood	10.8	12.9	12.7	12.9	15.9	12.8	12.0	12.85
Measuring, scientific, photographic equipment	12.6	12.9	14.9	15.0	16.1	17.1	15.6	14.88
Food	13.1	12.8	13.2	13.7	14.4	14.5	14.4	13.72
Toys, sporting goods	N/A	11.9	11.2	10.9	12.1	12.6	9.2	11.32
Glass, concrete, abrasives	8.3	11.9	11.9	13.9	14.0	11.3	9.6	11.55
Office equipment (includes computers)	10.4	11.5	12.7	15.7	15.9	15.1	13.3	13.51
Apparel	4.4	11.2	12.2	15.6	15.6	12.8	16.2	12.57
Textiles	5.4	10.7	8.8	11.2	11.7	8.1	7.8	9.10
Metal manufacturing	8.1	7.8	6.4	10.4	15.6	12.9	12.4	10.51
Rubber, plastic goods	8.8	7.3	11.4	10.7	8.2	5.0	10.4	8.82
All industries	11.6	13.3	13.5	14.3	15.9	14.4	13.8	13.82

Source: Reprinted by permission from *Fortune Magazine*, "The 500 Largest U.S. Industrial Companies," (Annual Survey, 1975, 1976, 1977, 1978, 1979, 1980, 1981).

Definition: Net income divided by book value of equity and reserves.

incentives (for example, stock relief in the United Kingdom), you need to find out the underlying profitability of the marketing and production parts of the business. After all, tax and financing decisions (that is, choices between debt and equity) are not dependent on the competitive market position or the efficiency of a firm's production, and it is the latter two that you need to know to assess business risk. In constructing the ratio, you should:

1. Include operating income (but not extraordinary income), investment income, and equity income.
2. Exclude the cost of short-term as well as long-term debt.
3. Capitalize any leases as assets, and, if possible, adjust operating income for the interest element in the lease payments.

Notice how it is possible for companies to improve return on equity by increasing their leverage, even though EBIT/TA remains unchanged.

Example 5.3. In 19X8, Hexagon had EBIT of $1,000 on assets of $8,000. There were no interest charges, and there was a tax rate of 50%. EBIT/TA was 12.5%, and the resulting net income was $500. Since owner's equity was $6,000, return on equity $500/$6,000, or 8.33%. (There was $2,000 of non-interest-bearing current liabilities, such as accounts payable.) In 19X9, Hexagon raised additional debt of $3,000 at an average interest cost of 8%. Total assets are now $11,000. EBIT/TA remains constant at 12.5%, producing EBIT of $1,375: After deduction of interest of $240, which is tax deductible, net income after tax is $567.5 and thus return on equity is 9.46%.

Hexagon's return on equity is higher because of leverage. It remains for the market to decide whether the introduction of debt makes the quality of earnings riskier. This depends on a number of variables which are not relevant to this example. If the stock market perceives Hexagon to be riskier than before, the required return on equity may rise to reflect this. As a credit analyst, however, you should be concerned more with any changes in EBIT/TA reflecting *operating* performance, since the loan has to be repaid with cashflow from operations.

LEVERAGE RATIOS

As has already been observed, the addition of debt or leverage improves return on equity for shareholders. Analysts must been keenly interested in the amount of leverage, and there have been a few attempts to devise golden rules as to how much debt a firm can have. For the moment, the suggested rule of thumb is simply to state that high leverage can only be justified by expectation of *reliable* cash flows.

Leverage increases profitability at the bottom line for two reasons: First, interest is tax deductible; second, the cost of debt to a firm is always less than the cost of equity, since lenders assume less risk than investors because they have prior claims on cashflow, both as to servicing their capital, and as to repayment in liquidation. Even if debt costs increase substantially because lenders perceive increased riskiness, the cost of equity in such situations must by definition (greater risk expects greater return) be higher.

Traditionally, debt has been measured by three ratios:

Debt/equity (debt/net worth)
Total liabilities/cash flow
Debt service coverage ratios

Each of these will now be examined in turn.

Debt/Equity (Debt/Net Worth)

There are differences of opinion as to the construction of this ratio. There are also differences of opinion as to its name. Let's deal first with terminology. Frequently, and regrettably, this ratio is referred to as the "debt/worth ratio." *Worth* by itself is not generally accepted as describing owner's equity. *Net worth* is sometimes so accepted, although it is more commonly used in the phrase *tangible net worth,* by which is meant all the owner's equity accounts minus any intangible assets. By reason of general usage, *equity* is usually regarded as meaning "owner's invested funds." So, our first step should be to prefer the phrasing "debt/equity ratio."

Next is a more difficult problem. Are we concerned here with all forms of debt or liability, or only with those forms that carry a financial cost? Does that financial cost mean interest, or does it include opportunity costs, such as the cost of discounts not obtained from suppliers (in which case accounts payable should be included as debt)?

The solution to the problem lies in considering the purpose of this measurement. As usual, the ratio—and indeed the problem—cannot be viewed in isolation. What we want to measure is the amount of total liabilities in relation to owner's equity so that we can see how much the business is built on owner's capital and how much on other people's money.

There's an old saying that OPM + PMA (other people's money plus a positive mental attitude) leads to riches. As a lender, you want to know the extent of the risks born by your bank and other lenders compared with the risks carried by the owners. Other people's money is always fine for the smart operator, but as a member of the "other people" who provide the money, you must be concerned with the extent to which you and other lenders bear the risks and the smart operator gets the rewards.

Following this line of argument, then, it makes sense to compare total liability to owner's equity in calculating the debt/equity ratio, even though some liabilities are noninterest bearing. It is not the cost of using other people's money that concerns us here; it is the amount. It will also be necessary to resolve questions as to whether to include deferred taxes in liabilities and minority interest in equity, and whether to deduct intangibles from owner's equity in order to use tangible net worth as the base. Once again, thinking about how the ratio can be used will help us answer these questions. Remember that a debt/equity ratio helps show by how much the assets could contract in value before the creditors' money is at risk or lost. This is illustrated by an example.

Example 5.4. Here we construct a "liquidation approach" debt/equity ratio. Jack Jones has the following consolidated balance sheet:

Cash	$ 5	Bank Debt	$ 15
Inventory	40	Accrued Liabilities	38
Accounts Receivable	60	Accounts Payable	32
Net Plant	130	Current Taxation	22
Trade Investments	70	Deferred Taxation[1]	27
Intangible Assets	20	Minority Interests	5
		Preferred Stock	45
		Owner's Equity	141
	325		325

All the liabilities are compared to all of the equity interests. The debt/equity ratio is

$$\frac{15 + 38 + 32 + 22 + 27}{5 + 45 + 141} = \frac{134}{191} = 0.70$$

Assets could contract in value from 325 to 134 before creditors were no longer covered by available assets—that is, a reduction in value of 191, or 58.77%. Of course, if this happened, preferred stock and owner's equity would probably be worthless. But we already know that they rank after the claims of creditors in a liquidation. Hence, that is why this is normally called a "liquidation approach" debt/equity ratio (see Chapter 6).

A few observations follow. Note that deferred taxes are treated as liabilities, since in a liquidation these taxes are likely to become currently due and payable. However, when one constructs a debt/equity ratio on a going concern basis, it is a common practice to leave deferred taxes out of both liabilities and equity calculations. Strictly speaking, this cannot be correct. Either deferred taxes are liabilities, or they are owner's reserves. Examination

[1]Arising from the fact that Jack Jones used rapid depreciation for tax purposes, but not for financial accounting.

of how the deferred taxes are created and the time span over which they will become due should help resolve the issue.

Note also that intangible assets were not deducted in this construction. This was because we had no information on the nature of these assets. Other practices assume a more conservative approach and deduct intangible assets from owner's equity to get tangible net worth. It seems better to say; "We want to know by how much assets could contract in value." Of course, some will fetch more than book value, some less, and some will have no value at all. But to assume that intangible assets are worthless seems unreasonable, given that we do not know anything about them or the other recorded book values. For instance, are fixed assets at historic cost (less depreciation) based on prices of 20 years ago? If so, market values for land and buildings will be seriously understated.

A final observation: Since minority interests are by definition equity investors in a consolidated business, it seems logical to group them with equity.

The debt/equity ratio is normally used by lenders to limit the risk to which their loans are exposed. Therefore, they require that the proportion of equity to total assets in a business be consistent with the risk level inherent in the assets that have been so financed. As a result, in term loan agreements (see Chapter 9), the debt/equity ratio is of vital importance and is frequently incorporated in the borrower's financial covenants, breach of which would lead to an Event of Default. It is in these situations that the ratio is usually expressed as "total liabilities/tangible net worth."

So the next question must be: How can one assess the risk level inherent in the assets? Only if this can be answered satisfactorily can a judgment be made as to whether a debt/equity ratio is good or bad. And the answer lies in the capacity of the current assets to be converted into cash through the normal course of business operations and, to a lesser extent, in the form of a fallback position the marketability of the fixed assets which could be sold to generate cash if they cannot support a good cash from operations position. That is to say, the risk level of assets is determined by their ability to generate cash on a *reliable basis*.

Once more we return to cashflow, rather than income, as the basis for assessing debt capacity. This time, however, it must be stressed that stability of cashflow is just as important as the amount of cashflow. Debt/equity ratios as they existed in certain U.S. industrial sectors in 1978 are shown in Table 5.2. From this, one may observe that some industries are much more leveraged than others. In theory, one would expect that this would reflect the stability of cash from operations in those industries. While this may be true for utilities, conglomerates, service industries, and tobacco, it seems that the marketability of assets rather than reliability of cashflow supported debt in the airlines industry.

There are definitely flaws in the debt/equity ratio. In summary, these are that it does not measure anything to do with cashflow; that book values of assets in a liquidation are never achieved, so the "asset contraction" ar-

Table 5.2 Debt Ratios of Selected U.S. Industry Sectors as of September 1978

	Percentage Short-Term Debt	Percentage Long-Term Debt	Percentage Equity	Debt/Equity Ratio
Real estate, housing	29.0	39.8	31.2	2.25
Airlines	4.3	54.3	41.4	1.47
Utilities	4.2	47.1	48.7	1.05
Conglomerates	9.4	40.0	50.6	0.97
Food and hotels	2.7	45.6	51.7	0.93
Service industries	9.8	36.8	53.4	0.87
Food retailing	3.8	42.1	54.1	0.85
Tobacco	6.8	34.6	58.6	0.70
Railroads	3.4	37.6	59.0	0.69
Department stores	15.5	25.5	59.0	0.69
Tires	9.1	31.2	59.7	0.69
Metals and mining	3.7	33.6	62.7	0.59
Chemicals	5.4	31.1	63.5	0.57
Steel	2.8	33.5	63.7	0.57
Appliances	9.6	25.3	65.1	0.54
Paper	2.0	30.1	67.9	0.47
Packaging	4.2	26.7	69.1	0.44
Machinery	8.4	21.6	70.0	0.42
Textiles	6.5	23.5	70.0	0.42
Beverages	2.9	21.6	75.5	0.32
Drugs	7.8	15.8	76.4	0.32
All industries	5.5	32.3	62.2	0.61

Source: Business Week, October 16, 1978, based on percentage of invested capital. Reprinted by permission.

gument is questionable; and that all of a company's liabilities are not shown on balance sheets as debt (for example, contingent liabilities, pensions, and lease commitments). However, since the ratio is so widely used, perhaps I should explain why it is important despite its weaknesses. The main reason is that lenders are keen to limit the total amount of debt that borrowers can undertake, since obviously adding debt to a company increases the claims on a company's cashflow and thus increases the riskiness of existing loans. A secondary reason may be that it is easy to calculate and thus to use as a basis of comparison between companies in the same industry. Remember that ratios are generally usefully calculated only when comparing like with like, and that what we want is a set of ratios that taken together will tell us something about our borrower compared with his competition. Debt/equity ratios will be significant in ranking competitors in an industry, since the financially strongest will usually be the least leveraged, and in being so, a company has more ability to undertake bold moves in strategic terms. Highly leveraged companies, on the other hand, in general have far less room to maneuver since mistakes will be more costly to them in weakening their financial condition and perhaps precipitating their collapse. Remember, too, that the more debt a company has, the less it is able to make independent decisions.

Cashflow/Total Liabilities

Recognizing the importance of cashflow to lenders, and the fact that debt/equity ratios do not take cashflow into account, we now turn to consider the use of cashflow/total liabilities as a measure of leverage. As is stated elsewhere (see Chapter 8), this ratio has been found by Beaver and others to be a very useful indicator of future financial problems in a firm.

Ideally, the ratio should consider all liabilities and compare them with cash from operations, rather than with net income plus noncash charges (that is, traditional gross cashflow), since it is cash from operations that will be available to repay the liabilities. In practice, gross cashflow is often used as the base instead.

A good ratio will depend both on the stability of future cashflows and on the level of interest rates. One way of looking at this is to consider an extreme case:

Example 5.5. A real estate company whose sole asset is one building has leased this to a government agency at a net $10,000 per annum for five years, after providing for all operating costs and taxes. If there are definitely no other calls on this "risk-free" cashflow (on the basis that the government agency will not default on the lease), the maximum amount that could be borrowed on this project will be the present value of these cashflows. This present value will be dependent on the interest rate used in discounting the cashflows, but at 10% with rentals payable annually in advance, the figure at the date of the signature of the lease (and the receipt of the first payment) would be $31,700 for the four remaining payments. This must by definition be true, since the present value sum represents exactly the amount that can be borrowed with annual repayments of $10,000 to cover capital and interest at 10%. Note that, if the market value of the building were to be the basis of the amount of the loan, implying that the sale of the building would be the source of the loan's repayment, a different debt maximum would be possible, based on the degree of certainty of the future sale price as well as interest rates.

Example 5.6. The Megan Company considers buying a machine for $75,000 with no resale market value because of its specialized use. This machine will produce expected net cashflows (that is, after all costs and taxes) from labor savings in production of $20,000 per annum for five years. Cashflows have been adjusted to "expected" levels based on probabilities estimated by management. After five years, the machine will be scrapped. Assuming a 10% interest rate and that the cashflows occur at the end of each period—

to make calculation easier—what is the amount which could be borrowed on these facts?

The present value of an annuity of $20,000 per annum for five years at 10% is 3.791 × $20,000 = $75,820. A lot depends on the probabilities estimated by management. In theory, it follows, that $75,820 would be the maximum debt to be supported by these cashflows alone. If this were done, however, the Megan Company would receive only $820 benefit from the machine, since the expected cashflow savings thus created would be almost entirely used up in repaying the debt required to purchase the machine. It would not, therefore, be likely to borrow $75,000 on these facts. Nor would a banker be willing to lend 100% of the purchase price of a machine! In practice, either the purchase price would be lower or the cashflows greater for such a financing.

Notice also that if the Megan Company did proceed to borrow $75,000, it would be increasing operating leverage[2] and financial leverage at the same time, which is a highly risky thing to do. Thus, it seems clear that the degree of future certainty of cashflows will influence the amount of debt which they can support.

This discussion has so far focused on debt that will be repaid by cashflows from operations. However, debt substitution may also be possible, given reasonable reliability of future cashflow. Indeed, this happens all the time with loans to finance companies and with interbank deposit placements. However, it is important at this stage to reflect on the total liabilities/cashflow ratio by itself. The question to consider is this: Is it possible to state generally what an acceptable ratio will be?

Once again, present value analysis should help us gain some perspective. Presented below is an extract from the present value of an annuity table, which can be found in many finance textbooks.

Years	6%	8%	10%	12%	14%	16%
1	.943	.926	0.909	0.893	0.877	0.862
2	1.833	1.783	1.736	1.690	1.647	1.605
3	2.673	2.577	2.487	2.402	2.322	2.246
4	3.465	3.312	3.170	3.037	2.914	2.798
5	4.212	3.993	3.791	3.605	3.433	3.274
6	4.917	4.623	4.355	4.111	3.889	3.685
7	5.582	5.206	4.868	4.564	4.288	4.039
8	6.210	5.747	5.335	4.968	4.639	4.344

[2]Operating leverage reflects the proportion of fixed costs to total costs: The more fixed costs it has, the more vulnerable a company is to a decline in revenues leading to operating losses. Operating leverage is a very important concept but unfortunately cannot be determined from financial statements.

In the first column, the figure 6.210 indicates that the present value of $1 received annually in arrears over eight years at 6% interest is today $6.21. Or put another way $6.21 of debt at 6% can be repaid at the rate of $1 per annum over a period of eight years.

Suppose we expect interest rates to be 10% and that we regard five years as the limit to the reasonably foreseeable business outlook. If cashflows remain constant, then liabilities of $3.791 can be repaid for every $1 of cashflow. This requires, of course, that these cashflows are not needed for other purposes (for example, capital investment). Perhaps a better way to estimate the ratio would be to estimate available cashflow after provision for capital expenditure.

By inspecting the table, we can see that a ratio greater than four requires either an outlook of more than five years or interest rates below 10%. That is to say if liabilities are more than four times cash flow, it will take longer than the foreseeable future (five years) to repay these, and/or it will depend on interest rates being less than 10% throughout the entire period. Whether this is realistic, is up to the banker to judge. In fact, many lenders consider that total long-term liabilities should not exceed four times gross cashflow. You should be cautious, however, about applying any number as a maximum figure for several reasons:

1. While total liabilities/cashflow is normally based on gross cashflow, some expenditure will be necessary for capital.
2. The table assumes constant cashflows. This is generally not realistic because of inflation.
3. The table is far less sensitive to interest rates than it is to the period of years being considered. Hence, the decision about what time horizon is reasonable for projections has a major effect on the outcome—that is, on what is an acceptable ratio.

Of course, you should remember that most liabilities are replaced as they are repaid in a continuing business. All that we are examining by using the present value of annuity table is the conceptual basis for choosing a maximum number, such as four times.

Debt Service Coverage Ratios

Debt service coverage ratios relate reported income to interest-bearing debt. These are popular with bond holders and with agencies that rate bonds for investors according to safety of principal and interest.

The simplest ratio is earnings before interest and taxes/interest payments. This is calculated using earnings before interest and taxes because interest is tax deductible. A ratio of less than 2, indicating that interest payments are only twice covered by available funds, would be cause for alarm. Unfortunately, the ratio uses earnings before interest and taxes rather than cash flow, so it is not adjusted for noncash charges.

A more advanced ratio would include lease payments, sinking fund payments, and all other forms of debt service required and would compare these with earnings before tax and depreciation. Adjustment would have to be made for capital repayments that are not tax deductible.

Both of these ratios are useful where debt substitution is likely to be the method of repayment for existing lenders. The ratios are also useful in that they relate current dollar interest payments to current dollar income rather than to historic cost debt; debt figures in terms of original capital amounts are distorted by inflation.

LIQUIDITY/SOLVENCY RATIOS

Many books on financial analysis frequently confuse liquidity and solvency. The ratios normally used to examine these features are the current ratio, the quick ratio, receivable turnover, inventory turnover, and net working assets/sales. While these can all be useful, it pays to know what you are measuring.

In this book, *liquidity* means "nearness to cash." *Solvency* means "ability to pay one's debts as they fall due." Frequently, a high ratio of current assets to current liabilities (a high current ratio) is described as showing a strong liquid position. Of course, that is not strictly true, since the definition of current assets includes work in progress, which may be very illiquid because of the length of the production process, and accounts receivable, where extended credit of up to three years may be granted. It all depends on the composition of those assets and liabilities and the degree to which cash demands can be met from cash resources, including undrawn short-term lines of credit. An illiquid firm can be solvent if it has the ability to borrow to pay its debts even though its assets are not near to being turned into cash. And a liquid firm could become insolvent if its combined liabilities (including its long-term debt) exceed its assets, even though the current assets are mostly cash and exceed its short-term liabilities. The trigger would be a default on a covenant in a term debt agreement that resulted in all debt becoming immediately payable.

The current ratio is, then, the simplest and most traditional method for measuring liquidity. Even though it has drawbacks, the ratio shows that any firm whose current ratio is less than unity is at first glance unable to meet its current obligations out of its current assets. Further investigation is then necessary to determine the nature of the lack of liquidity and the extent of the liabilities. Such a company would perhaps be a company that owned apartment blocks where the rental income to be received in the future would easily repay the current liabilities. Admittedly, however, such firms are rare, and manufacturing companies with current ratios of less than one are generally poor credit risks.

The quick ratio is also used to measure liquidity and consists of current assets, exclusive of the investment in inventory, compared with current liabilities. Where inventory or work in progress is substantial, this may be a more useful ratio than the current ratio.

Inventory levels are measured in terms of days of inventory on hand, and accounts receivable are measured in terms of days of sales represented by the amount of receivables outstanding. Changes in these numbers from year to year should be examined and explained. Care should be taken, however, to look for changes in the product mix of the company that can explain changes in these numbers. The formula for finding the ratio is

$$\frac{\text{Inventory}}{\text{Cost of goods sold}} \times 365$$

and this will tell you days of inventory on hand. This is discussed further in the next chapter. Similarly, days of receivables can be found thus:

$$\frac{\text{Accounts receivable}}{\text{Sales}} \times 365$$

And days of payables thus:

$$\frac{\text{Accounts payable}}{\text{Cost of goods sold}} \times 365$$

These three items can be combined to find the number of days in the cash cycle, which is discussed in Chapter 3.

The Self-financing Short-Term Growth Rate

As we have seen, net working assets as a percentage of sales can be looked on as the ratio to use to find out how much of an increase there will be next year in such items as inventory, receivables, and payables that taken together will reduce gross funds flow (that is, net income plus depreciation) to an actual figure for cash from operations. You can also use the net margin on sales to find the amount of funds generated by the profit margin on sales. Then combining these two, you can find the level to which the company can grow in the next period without having to increase short-term debt to cover an additional requirement for an increase in net working assets. In fact, it is possible to refer to the net working assets/sales ratio as the cash efficiency ratio and the profit margin as the cash-generating ratio.

In Exhibit 5.2, Paragon has a current sales level of $3,000, with a profit margin of 8% and a ratio of net working assets/sales of 20%. At a sales level in the next period that is constant at $3000, funds from operations will be $240 and no additional net working assets will be needed, thus cash from operations will also be $240. At a sales level of $4,000, funds from operations

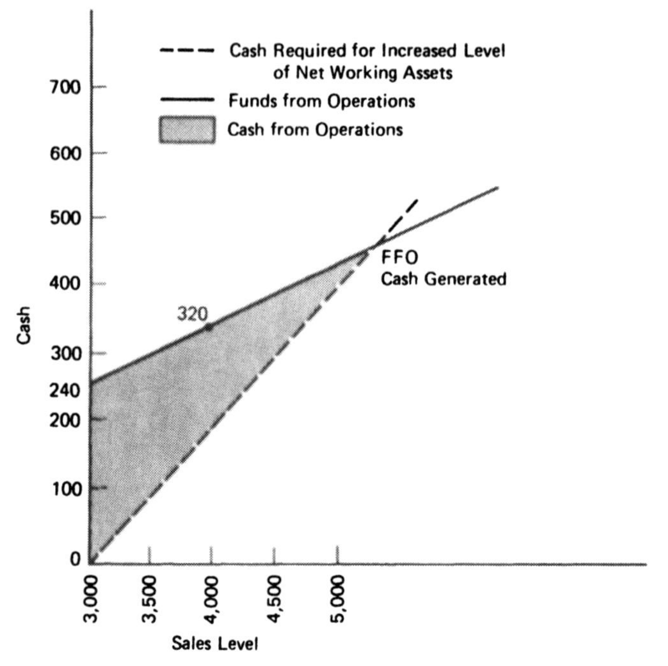

Exhibit 5.2 The Self-Financing Growth Rate, Paragon.

will be \$320 (8% of \$4,000) and net working assets will have to increase by 20% of the difference in sales levels (20% of \$1,000), hence cash from operations will be \$120. In fact, all of the shaded area will be positive cash from operations. At a sales level of \$5,000, funds from operations will be \$400 (8% of \$5,000), but since sales are now \$2,000 greater than the former level, Paragon will need \$400 (20% of \$2,000) more in net working assets. As can be seen, sales increases of less than this level are self-financing, whereas those above will produce negative cash from operations.

This model has several very limiting assumptions. Mostly these relate to economies of scale, operating leverage, and so on. It is probably not credible that the profit margin would remain constant with such sharp increases in sales, but the concept can be useful for seeing the extent to which increases in net working assets can be internally financed by profit margins. Note also that the profit margin excludes depreciation expense.

Generalizing, where p is the profit margin and q is the net working assets/sales ratio, the self-financing growth rate x is

$$x = \frac{p}{q - p}$$

PERFORMANCE RATIOS

Each industry has performance ratios in terms of the efficient use of assets. These ratios concentrate on the assets that are the most significant to that industry. Significance is most often determined by cost, especially where high operating leverage is present. That is to say, if an asset gives rise to a high level of fixed costs and thus to high operating leverage, it makes sense to relate sales revenues to the size of this asset.

For example, in hotels, the normal performance ratio is an occupancy ratio measured as the proportion of bedrooms filled each night, since it is these rooms that govern the amount of fixed costs. In the airlines industry, one ratio used to measure operating efficiency is the revenue passenger load factor (RPLF). Because of the high element of fixed costs, the higher the RPLF, the better the performance. RPLF is found by dividing the number of revenue passenger-miles flown by the number of available seat-miles flown. Such factors as route structure, aircraft type, and seat configuration should be taken into account and the airline compared with others of its type. Another efficiency measure is total operating expense per available seat-mile. Total operating expense generally increases with the size of the aircraft, but greater capacity usually results in lower operating expense per available seat-mile. In electric utilities, costs per unit of output are important. In retailing, sales per square foot of selling space is used. As analysts, you are advised to develop your own performance ratios to cover the industries in which you are interested, bearing in mind the data that companies disclose that can be used for comparative analysis.

SUMMARY ON USING FINANCIAL RATIOS

Single financial ratios suffer from some disadvantages in computation but are important for comparative purposes. Multiratios (that is, equations using several ratios with appropriate constants) can be very important for determining trends, especially in predicting corporate collapse, and are discussed in Chapter 8.

The following chapter on financial condition discusses how to use financial ratios and performance ratios in practice. Analysts must always remember how ratios fit together and how one set of ratios will affect another set. For example, higher leverage ratios can produce higher return on equity. Exhibit 5.3 illustrates this.

In this example, the company's balance sheet and income statement are as follows:

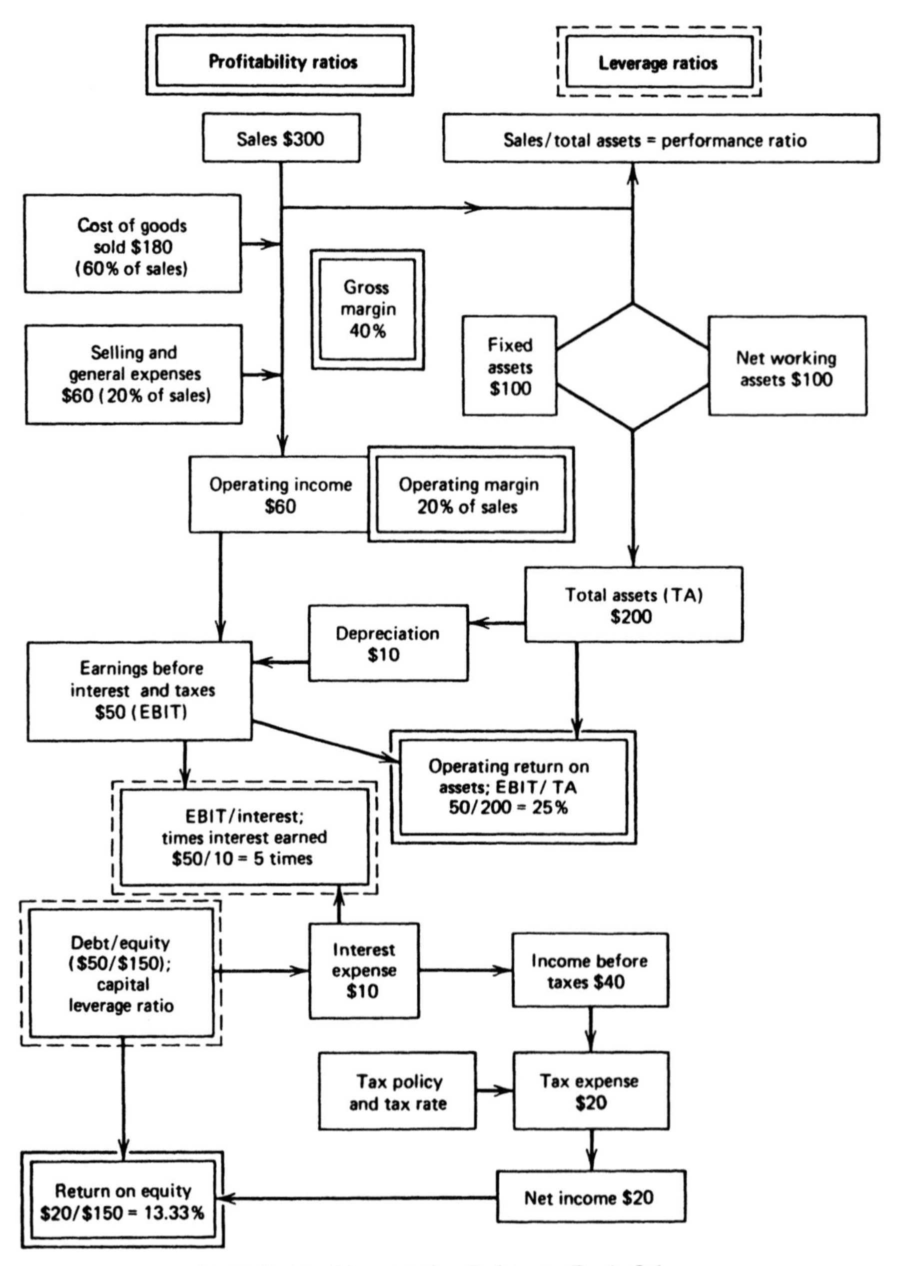

Exhibit 5.3 How Ratios Relate to Each Other

Balance Sheet

NWA	$100	Debt	$ 50
Fixed Assets	100	Equity	150
	$200		$200

Income Statement

Sales	$300
Cost of Goods Sold	180
Selling and General Expense	60
Depreciation	10
Interest Expense	10
Income before Taxes	40
Tax Expense	20
Net Income	20

Note that if Debt was not $50 but $80, Equity would be $120, Interest Expense would be $16, Net Income would be $17, and hence Return on Equity would be 17/120 = 14.16%.

PROBLEM

Attempt the industry identification exercise that follows:

Everyone knows that there are variations in operational and financial policies and practices and in operating results between firms in the same industry. However, the nature of each industry has an important impact on the general patterns of asset allocation as well as on the financial results of most firms in the industry. Presented in Exhibit 5.4 are balance sheets, in percentage form, and selected ratios drawn from the balance sheets and operating statements of 11 firms in 11 different U.S. industries as of December 31, 1979. Recognizing the fact of certain differences between firms in the same industry, each firm whose figures are summarized is broadly typical of those in its industry. In fact, all but the first named have debt which is rated A by Moody's Industrial Services. Here are the 11 industries:

1. Fast-food chain
2. Electric utility
3. Supermarket chain
4. Broadcasting and movie producer
5. Regional domestic airline

Exhibit 5.4 Industry Identification Exercise

	A	B	C	D	E	F	G	H	I	J	K
Cash	13.2	3.1	4.8	6.5	—	15.0	1.3	4.4	5.2	16.7	3.7
Receivables	3.5	2.0	8.0	37.1	4.9	12.9	22.6	23.3	25.6	21.3	16.3
Inventory	3.3	31.6	39.7	19.2	2.8	3.2	28.5	8.9	22.6	1.7	34.3
Other	1.2	2.2	1.1	1.1	1.0	3.6	1.2	0.5	—	16.6	1.3
Plant and equipment	78.1	60.4	28.1	33.4	87.7	47.3	42.5	58.3	28.8	23.5	24.3
Other assets	0.7	0.7	18.1	2.7	3.6	18.0	3.9	5.5	17.8	20.2	20.1
Total	100	100	100	100	100	100	100	100	100	100	100
Notes payable	—	0.6	1.5	5.5	2.1	5.0	4.1	2.6	1.7	1.0	13.9
Accounts payable	16.8	28.1	15.1	14.5	2.3	17.0	15.9	21.9	6.5	4.1	—
Other accruals	—	—	4.0	—	2.9	7.3	—	1.0	15.2	13.4	—
Current taxes	2.2	0.1	2.6	2.5	—	1.0	4.8	8.6	3.7	3.4	3.9
Long-term debt	7.6	30.8	12.5	16.0	44.9	29.4	27.2	19.8	13.1	17.7	25.9
Other long-term liabilities (including preferred stock)	1.8	1.6	5.3	4.2	18.7	8.8	7.5	15.3	10.6	1.0	2.6
Owner's equity	71.6	38.8	59.0	57.3	29.1	31.5	40.5	30.8	49.2	62.8	53.7
Total	100	100	100	100	100	100	100	100	100	100	100
Net income	10.5	1.04	6.1	1.0	11.5	4.6	1.7	5.8	6.1	7.7	5.1
Return on equity	28.5	14.2	17.5	17.9	11.3	15.4	6.7	41.8	15.8	20.9	12.9
Sales/total assets	1.91	4.42	1.62	10.9	0.28	1.36	1.53	1.74	1.26	1.61	1.40

6. Meat packer
7. Engineering equipment
8. Large electronics company
9. Rubber tire maker
10. Tobacco manufacturer
11. Oil company

Now match the industry with the firm. For instance, if column A is the supermarket chain, write A3 and give reasons.

Appendix 1 Case Studies

CASE STUDY 1: KWAI LAM ELECTRONICS

In the spring of 1979, Harry Jackson, assistant vice president of Commercial Bank of California's (CBC) Taipei Branch, was considering a request from one of Taiwan's emerging growth companies for a credit line of $3 million. This company, Kwai Lam Electronics (KLE), had been a prospect for CBC Taipei for the past two years, but this opportunity represented the first real chance of doing business with them. KLE was the eighth largest member of the industry and was principally engaged in making color TVs and transistor radios.

ELECTRONICS INDUSTRY IN TAIWAN

The development of the electronics industry over the past decade has shown a rapid rise, as indicated both by increase in production as well as growth of exports. In 1977, the total annual production value of the electronic and electric appliance industry reached US$2.01 billion, increasing nearly 10 times over 1968. Exports jumped by almost 17 times during a similar period, rising from US$79 million to US$1.48 billion to account for 15.81% of Taiwan's total exports for 1977, next only to the textile industry. As the electronic and electric appliance industry continues to exhibit strong growth for the first half of 1978, it is expected that before 1981, when the current six-year economic plan is completed, the industry will replace the textile industry as the largest exporting industry. This is because the future of Taiwan's textile industry is gloomy because of problems of overcapacity, weak demand both at home and abroad, and growing competition from Southeast Asian countries, South Korea, and possibly the People's Republic of China. On the other hand, local industrialists maintain that the prospect of Taiwan's electronic and electric appliance industry is bright in spite of the import quota restriction on color TV exports imposed by the United States effective February 1, 1979. CBC Taipei's outstandings to 11 electronic and electric appliance manufacturers increased 59.7% from US$10.6 million as of January 1978 to US$16.9 million as of January 1979, representing 14.8% of the total loan portfolio as of January 1979, versus 7.4% as of January 1978.

It is anticipated that the loan demand will continue to increase from this industry mainly because total sales of CBC customers accounted for 22% (on an average) of total electronic and electric appliance sales on this island for the past three years, while their total exports accounted for only 9% (on an average) of Taiwan's exports over the same period. Consequently, it was thought that a study of the structure, the growth potential, and the future trends of this industry could enable CBC to formulate a marketing as well as risk strategy.

History

Since 1947 Taiwan has had the ability to produce electric fans and radios, although the quality of these products was not good. However, the first major progressive step was the establishment of the Taiwan Television Corp. in 1962, which started local assembly of TV. The establishment of Taiwan General Instrument Corp. in 1964 by the General Instrument Corp. of the United States has led an impressive and continuous inflow of foreign capital investment into Taiwan's electronic and electric appliance industry. With the abundant cheap and skilled labor force, and the favorable investment environment supported by the infrastructure—namely, transportation systems, communication channels, electric power, industrial complexes, and export processing zones—the electronic and electric appliance industry in Taiwan has made tremendous progress and become the fastest growing industry in Taiwan during the past decade. The Japanese yen's appreciation of 32% over the past 12 months and a high rate of domestic price inflation in South Korea has prompted the foreign buyers to switch their purchase from Japan and South Korea to Taiwan. As a result, the pace of growth of the Taiwan electronic and electric appliance industry has accelerated.

In the late 1970's, there were 1,160 firms engaged in the manufacture of electronic and electric appliance products, of which 858 were owned by local investors, 50 exclusively by foreign investors (mainly U.S. companies), with the remaining 252 being joint ventures. Although the number of foreign firms and joint ventures is far less than that of local firms, the role of these firms in the development of Taiwan's electronic and electric appliance industry is significant—mainly in terms of production scale and the quality of their products. Over 60% of total industry sales is contributed by only 25 companies (see Exhibit A1.1).

Electronic Appliances

The electronic products made in Taiwan include video and audio products, and are mainly televisions (both black and white and color), digital watches, electronic calculators, telephones and switchboards, transistor radios, and sound systems. A brief review of past supply and demand as well as the prospects for television production is given below, followed by a brief discussion of the other major sectors of the industry.

Exhibit A1.1 Industry Figures

In terms of 1977 sales, the leading companies in Taiwan in electronic and electric appliances were (figures in US $ Millions):

1.	Tatung*	200.2
2.	Matsushita Electric (Taiwan)	108.3
3.	Sampo*	106.6
4.	RCA Taiwan*	101.1
5.	Sanyo Electric Taiwan	88.8
6.	Texas Instrument Taiwan	65.3
7.	Admiral Overseas Corp.	55.0
8.	Kwai Lam Electronics	50.3
9.	TECO Electric*	50.0
10.	Capetronic (Taiwan)	45.2

*CBC Taipei has relationships with those marked with an asterisk.

Note. The top 25 companies account for 64% of the total industry sales.

Exhibit A1.2 Summarized Financial Statements, Kwai Lam Electronics, 1978 (in NT $ million)

	1976	1977	1978
Cash	12	2	10
Receivables	462	504	880
Inventory	796	890	1,247
Advances to Suppliers	60	60	170
Other Current Assets	42	50	55
Total Current Assets	1,372	1,506	2,362
Net Fixed Assets	446	506	642
Investments			
Other Assets	34	46	50
Total Assets	1,852	2,058	3,054
Bank Debt	720	790	1,268
Other Current Liabilities	564	662	980
Long-Term Liabilities	158	130	150
Total Liabilities	1,442	1,582	2,398
Capital	336	348	398
Retained Earnings	74	128	258
Total Liabilities and Net Worth	1,852	2,058	3,054
Sales	1,870	2,105	3,450
Cost of Goods Sold	1,567	1,703	2,656.5
Gross Profit	303 (16.2%)	402 (19.1%)	793.5 (23%)
Depreciation	70	82	110
Other Expenses	183	141	373
Taxation	22	80	138
Net Income	28	99 (4.7%)	172.5 (5.0%)

Exhibit A1.3 Summarized Financial Statements of the Principal TV and Radio Companies in Taiwan (in NT $1 million)

	Tatung		Sampo		Teco	
	1976	1977	1976	1977	1976	1977
Cash	44	68	111	267	105	111
Receivables	1,462	1,947	691	922	277	390
Inventory	1,814	2,062	814	947	441	511
Advances to Suppliers	520	654	51	70	64	60
Other Current Assets	239	252	9	19	3	1
Total Current Assets	4,079	4,983	1,676	2,225	890	1,073
Net Fixed Assets	1,698	1,954	433	545	359	430
Investments	366	455	71	97	75	91
Other Assets	200	422	85	82	44	44
TOTAL ASSETS	6,343	7,814	2,265	2,949	1,368	1,637

Bank Debt	2,100	3,005	900	1,210	490	583
Other Current Liabilities	2,007	2,000	572	503	284	350
Total Current Liabilities	4,107	5,005	1,472	1,713	774	933
Long-Term Liabilities	427	487	143	379	13	27
Total Liabilities	4,534	5,492	1,615	2,092	787	960
Capital	1,124	1,657	395	550	330	400
Retained Earnings	685	665	255	307	251	277
TOTAL	6,343	7,814	2,265	2,949	1,368	1,637
Sales	5,366	7,600	3,055	4,050	1,587	1,900
Cost of Goods Sold	3,864	5,472	2,108	2,754	1,174	1,311
Gross Profit	1,502	2,128	947	1,296	413	589
Other Expenses	1,002.4	1,459.4	687.2	832.4	73.8	207.3
Depreciation	220	245	50	70	40	50
Taxes	124	188	92.9	174.9	131	147.4
NET INCOME	155.6	235.6	116.9	218.7	168.2	184.3

Note: NT $38 = US $1.

Television. As of 1979, Taiwan was the biggest producer and exporter of black and white TVs in the world. Total production reached 4,515,102 units in 1977, a jump of 35.7% over the previous year, and represented 22.6% of 1977's world black and white TV production. Of the total sales, 96.6% was for export, with only 3.4% for local consumption. This is because the saturation rate for black and white TVs in Taiwan had reached 90%, leaving very limited room for growth. In fact, of late, the sales of black and white TVs in Taiwan have shown a declining trend. Major exports have been to the United States (80%), Western Europe (7%), Central America (5.2%), and Southeast Asia (4.5%). Although the world demand for black and white TVs has declined continuously, Taiwan's exports in the first half of 1978 continued to show a big jump, up 41.5% over the same period in 1977. This is mainly because Taiwan's black and white TV manufacturers have a competitive edge in the international market in both price and quality. The growth is also attributed to the successful market promotion in Western Europe and Southeast Asia (Indonesia and Thailand), which uses the CCIR system instead of the U.S. system, as well as the introduction of such new products as the mini TV/recorder/radio, which has been widely accepted by the consumers.

The annual production growth rate for color TVs during 1974–1976 showed a 19.7% increase on average. Color TV exports as a percentage of total TV sales over this period, however, showed a declining trend, from 67.3% in 1974 to 45.6% in 1975 and 47.7% in 1976, mainly due to the fierce competition among color TV producers, especially from Japanese firms. Fortunately, the increase in domestic sales during this period, which can be attributed to the improved living standard and the preference for color TV, has partly cushioned the reduction in the growth rate of exports. However, the pace of color TV exports rapidly accelerated in the second half of 1977, with the U.S. quota against Japanese color TV exports in July[1] and the Japanese yen's appreciation. Local color TV manufacturers seized the opportunity presented by the U.S.–Japanese color TV orderly marketing agreement to expand exports to the United States. As a result, color TV exports increased from 238,784 units in 1976 to 563,302 units in 1977, representing a 135.9% increase versus a 50.7% increase in 1976. Color TV exports as a percentage of total sales thus increased sharply from 47.7% in 1976 to 63% in 1977. Local sales of color TVs in 1977 also increased sharply, from 261,838 units in 1976 to 330,776 units in 1977, or by 26.3%. This was mainly due to the continuing rise in per capita income. Color TV sales both at home and abroad continued and showed a big jump for the first half of 1978 to 207,279 and 507,137 units, respectively, representing a 37.5% and 156.7% increase, respectively, over the same period of the previous year. Listed on page 225 are the production and sales of TVs for 1974–1978.[2]

[1]This quota contract regulated that Japanese color TV exports, including chassis (that is, partially assembled color TVs, excluding picture tubes, speakers, and cabinets), to the United States, could not exceed 1.75 million units per year.

[2]From Taiwan Industrial Production Statistics Monthly, MOEA.

Black and White TV Sets

	Production	Percentage Change	Sales in Volume	Percentage Change	Local	Percentage Change	Export	Percentage Change
1974	3,617,746	−13.9	3,769,126	−8.9	277,977	−13.9	3,491,149	−8.5
1975	2,599,311	−28.2	2,641,246	−29.9	207,314	−25.4	2,433,932	−30.3
1976	3,326,432	27.9	3,556,352	34.7	152,922	−26.2	3,403,430	39.8
1977	4,515,102	35.7	4,027,923	13.3	135,229	−11.6	3,892,694	14.4
1978 (6 mos)	2,668,193	20.2*	2,406,267	39.1*	54,150	−18.4*	2,352,117	41.5*

Color TV Sets

	Production	Percentage Change	Sales in Volume	Percentage Change	Local	Percentage Change	Export	Percentage Change
1974	418,453	23.2	506,141	14.6	132,667	109.0	273,474	− 6.0
1975	335,661	−19.8	347,741	14.4	189,301	42.7	158,440	−42.1
1976	523,614	56.0	500,622	43.9	261,838	38.3	238,784	50.7
1977	910,589	73.9	894,078	78.6	330,776	26.3	563,302	135.9
1978 (6 mos)	802,646	125.5*	714,416	105.1*	207,279	37.5*	507,137	156.7*

*This represents a comparison with the same period of 1977.

Major manufacturers of black and white TVs and color TVs are as follows:

1. U.S.-controlled companies
   RCA Taiwan
   Zenith Taiwan
2. Japanese-controlled companies
   Matsushita Electric (Taiwan)
   Sanyo Electric (Taiwan)
   Hitachi Electric (Taiwan)
3. Local companies
   Tatung Co.
   Sampo Corp.
   Kwai Lam
   Taiwan Kolin
   United Electronics
   TECO Electric
4. Overseas Chinese-controlled company
   Admiral Overseas

Harry Jackson knew that the U.S. government had begun an import quota system against Taiwanese color TV exports in February 1979. According to the orderly marketing agreement signed in December 1978 by Taiwan and the United States, Taiwan was to be permitted to export 127,000 fully assembled color TVs between February and June 30, 1979, and 373,000 sets between July 1 and June 30, 1980. As regards chassis (partially assembled color TVs), Taiwan was to be permitted to export 270,000 between February 1 and June 30, 1979. Jackson thought that the above measure would undoubtedly adversely affect the development of the Taiwan color TV industry, as it was just in the pre-take-off stage. Although the export of color TVs to the United States in 1977 registered a high of 460,000 units (including chassis), only 181,000 units were made by three Taiwanese-owned firms (Tatung, Sampo, and Kwai Lam). U.S. and Japanese manufacturers, such as Admiral Overseas, RCA Taiwan, Zenith Taiwan, and Hitachi Electric Taiwan, set up as subsidiaries of their parent companies to escape skyrocketing labor costs at home, contributed the remaining color TV exports. Moreover, although the export of Taiwan-made color TVs to the United States started in early 1971, the history of the three Taiwanese-owned TV manufacturers started in the late 1970s. As a consequence, the quota system was most likely to affect adversely the development of the local color TV industry, as the allotment of quota in general was made on the basis of producers' past export records, and the three local manufacturers held only a 20% share of total color TV exports.

As a result of the development of this unfavorable condition for the local color TV industry, the Ministry of Economic Affairs announced (effective October 1, 1978) a ban on entry of Japanese firms to manufacture color TVs in Taiwan. Additionally, the Ministry had informed the local Japanese color TV producers to restrict their exports to the United States to the level of 1977. Market diversification to Western Europe, which used PAL system instead of NTSC system, appeared to be the best solution. However, even though the local manufacturers do not have the technology to produce color TVs with PAL system, the situation could change within a year or two because Grundig Taiwan plans to introduce PAL system, as the existing license for such a system, which is held by Telefunken Corporation, the patent holder, expires at the end of 1978.

Product diversification was also a possibility for this industry. Sampo and Kwai Lam were planning to produce more combination models of small-screen monochrome TV, radios, and cassette recorders, and other new products that are not subject to quotas. Also, the availability of a local supply of picture tubes made by Philips Taiwan since September 1978 should make local color TVs more competitive in international markets.

The prospect of local sales of color TVs was promising, as the saturation rate of this sector for home use was only 40% in 1979. As for black and white TVs, although the demand for this sector both at home and abroad was declining as a whole, it was expected that black and white TV sales in the near future will continue to be steady, provided that Taiwan producers could continue to maintain a competitive edge in international markets and produce a new style of black and white TV, such as a battery-powered portable TV, which is anticipated to replace the most popular 12-inch model to meet the consumers' demand.

Other Sectors. Other major sectors of the electronic and electric appliance industry, in which CBC has some important relationships are as follows:

Digital watches. Although only begun in 1975, the development of this sector has been spectacular. Production has increased from 284,000 units in May 1975 to 7.5 million units in 1978, and the number of participating firms from 8 to 30. Over 90% of output is exported. The industry uses imported components from Japan, and assembles and reexports principally to the United States. Growth is slowing as competition increases from Korea, Hong Kong, Japan, and Switzerland.

Electronic Calculators. From 1972–1977, production of calculators increased 81 times from 55,000 to 4.4 million sets, of which 92% was exported. Major producers are Tatung, Santron, Calcomp, and Logitech. Production in 1978 was 46% ahead of 1977. Taiwan has a labor cost advantage here over Hong Kong, Korea, and Japan, its principal competitors. Mostly operations are assembly of imported parts for subsequent reexport. Profits are low because of intense competition.

Telecom Equipment. In 1979, production was running 24.8% ahead of 1977, and much of this was sold locally. Owing to improvements in the domestic standard of living, Taiwan was now second in Asia only to Japan in telephone density, at 9.2 telephones per 100 persons. Locally made telephones account for 97% of domestic sales, and prospects are bright because this sector is not dependent on exports.

Audio Equipment. The transistor radio has been the flagship of Taiwan audio products. In the 1960s, components and parts were totally imported from abroad, mainly from Japan, and the radios were only assembled. By now in early 1979, the transistor radio industry manufactures 90% of components locally and exports 95% of its output, mostly to the United States, West Germany, Canada, and Japan. Growth had slowed recently because of intense competition from other industrializing Asian countries, such as Korea and Hong Kong. Production in 1978 exceeded 8 million units compared with 7 million in 1975. Prospects are good, as the industry produces new models, such as clock radios. Kwai Lam is the number three manufacturer of transistor radios, behind Tatung and Sampo.

"1978 turned out to be a boom year for our industry," said Mr. Wong, president of Kwai Lam, when Harry Jackson called on him in April 1979. "The main reason appears to be that we were able to grab a large share of the U.S. color TV import market, which previously was held by Japanese manufacturers. Our color TV exports were more than 100% ahead of 1977's figures and account for most of our overall sales gain of 63%." When questioned by Jackson about future prospects, Wong replied, "Of course competition is intensifying, but we expect further sales growth in 1979 in the United States, and our penetration of European markets, which is low at present, is expected to increase as soon as we are able to produce PAL sets. Sales of transistor radios will probably grow at about 10%, in line with industry forecasts."

Jackson pressed him about financing opportunities: "Of course, with all this growth, you'll be needing to add to your bank lines for financing inventory and other short-term assets." Wong confirmed that was true: "We are looking to add another bank to our inner group of four banks. I think you know we already use two local banks, as well as Chase and Bank of America. We use all these four banks for letter of credit and preexport financing."

Jackson knew that this meant the banks were willing to lend an amount of money equal to a fixed percentage of the recorded value of inventory and receivables to the subject company, provided that letters of credit existed to support export sales. Currently, CBC lent to another member of the electronics industry in Taiwan on the basis of 85% of receivables and 45% of inventory. He was wondering whether those figures would be acceptable to Kwai Lam.

In reply to his questions, Wong told him that their inventory figures typically consisted of 30% raw materials, 50% work in progress, and 20% finished goods. Most of the materials were locally produced, apart from TV tubes, which were imported from Japan. This was considered to be cheaper than making them in-house because of economies of scale in production. Sales were made principally to the large retailing groups, such as K-Mart, Sears Roebuck, and Macy's department stores, although 30% of U.S. sales were also made to an independent distributor, who sold to smaller specialized TV and radio shops.

HISTORY OF THE COMPANY

Kwai Lam Electronics (KLE) was founded in 1965 by Wong and his father-in-law K. L. Chen (after whom the company is named) with a small amount of capital. Over the next 10 years, they established themselves as a dominant feature in the transistor radio export market through a strategy of combining reliable quality with low profit margins but substantial volume. Thus, they penetrated well into the North American market and became suppliers to many large "own label" retailers. In 1974, the decision was taken to move into manufacture of color TVs, although KLE had previously avoided the black and white TV market completely. This proved to be a very successful move because of the marketing expertise already acquired and the fact that TV tubes, a major expense component, could be imported from Japan. Thus, assembly operations continued in Taiwan, with the goods destined for eventual reexport. KLE is privately owned by the Chen and Wong families, who controlled 88% of the shares. Wong, president, is 43 and was educated in Taiwan, although he attended the University of British Columbia Business School in the late 1960s, where he obtained an MBA.

TRADE FINANCING

Substantial volumes of trade all over the world are financed by means of letters of credit. In essence, a letter of credit is an instruction from a buyer's bank to a seller's bank to pay out money to the seller provided the seller can produce documents evidencing that the goods being sold meet the buyer's requirements, have been shipped, and are insured. Obviously, this is of vital importance to manufacturers dealing with buyers in foreign countries whose credit standing is unknown. In place of the unknown buyer, the seller is able to deal with a local bank, which the seller knows, and the bank in turn relies on the strength of the foreign bank (the buyer's bank), which will refund the local bank in exchange for the documents any money paid to the seller. In addition, documents include bills of lading, which represent title to the goods in question, giving both banks collateral over the goods in transit should the buyer fail to pay in the end. Thus, the credit risk of an opening bank (the buyer's bank) is that the buyer is not good for the money. The advising bank (the seller's bank) has the credit risk only of the foreign bank, and the seller is able to get his money when the goods are shipped.

KLE used letters of credit to pay for imports of TV tubes from Japan and

	1976		1977		1978	
	Units	Percentage of Total Sales	Units	Percentage of Total Sales	Units	Percentage of Total Sales
Color TVs	121,000	57.2	139,000	56.7	280,000	70.1
Radios	775,000	42.8	810,000	43.3	900,000	29.9

was paid through letters of credit opened by its foreign buyers through banks in Taipei for goods which it exported. However, with some of its customers of long standing, open account sales were made by KLE. These customers usually paid within 30 days of invoicing.

The sales split (home market and export sales together) between transistors and color TVs has been (see page 230):

As can be seen, the expansion of color TVs and their higher sales volume per unit has dramatically changed the sales mix of the company. "Seventy percent of our sales now [1978] are color TVs, and 92% of these are exported," said Wong. "In fact the United States accounted for 220,000 units of our production of TVs in 1978, and we hope to maintain this market share in 1979. As you can see, we are not in black and white television manufacture and really only began in color TVs in 1975. Our strategy has been to aim for high added value in this sector to compensate for the increased competition in transistor radios."

As Jackson reviewed the whole file, he wondered if this was really such a good prospect for CBC. The longer range expectations, however, of KLE's growth and the chance to obtain additional noncredit business appeared to offset some of the immediate difficulties in lending to the company.

CASE STUDY 2: SILMARAX S.A.

In March 1982, Silmarax S.A., a French company based in Chalons Sur Marne, was seeking bank financing for a $5 million five-year term loan to be used for capital expenditure in the older of its two plants in France. Jim Arlington, treasurer of Silmarax, who was on assignment from Silmarax's parent company, Melvin Corporation of Cleveland, Ohio, had originally decided to invite several banks to bid for the loan. He had narrowed the choice to Melvin's lead U.S. bank and also Banque Nationale de Paris, a nationalized French bank with whom Melvin did a lot of its French business, especially because the U.S bank's Paris office had limited ability to obtain French francs owing to government restrictions. BNP provided them with a FF 30 million line of credit.[1]

Silmarax was an old established firm engaged in making axles, transmissions, and other parts for trucks. The original owners had sold out for $20 million to Melvin Corporation in 1979, when Melvin was seeking to expand within the EEC and needed a larger base for manufacturing. Silmarax had two plants in northern France, one of which had extensive land available for building. Melvin had no other French subsidiaries, but its European companies included a plant for tractor engines in Italy, which supplied Fiat.

[1]FF 6.00 = U.S.$1.00 as at March 1, 1982.

Sales units were expected to grow between 3%—taking the most pessimistic view—and 15% per annum over the next five years. Jim Arlington's profit plan was based on 8% per annum volume growth and 7% per annum inflationary increases in costs and selling prices. Non-EEC exports were priced in U.S. dollars, but the rest of sales were priced in French francs. France is a member of the European Monetary System, which Arlington believed would be a steadying force in terms of possible fluctuations of EEC currencies. The term loan was to be in U.S. dollars because the machinery was to be purchased in the United States. Melvin Corporation would be willing to provide a comfort letter in the form shown in Exhibit A2.2. Arlington expected to be asked to agree to some financial covenants but had decided to wait until proposals were made to him from the two banks before making up his mind as to what was acceptable. As he waited for the two offers, he reflected that the BNP appeared very eager to do more business with Melvin, since so far it had dealt directly only with the French subsidiary. He had noticed some hesitation, however, on the part of the U.S. bank's Paris account officer, which he put down to inexperience, as the officer had apparently only just graduated from the bank's training program. Knowing that Martin B. Melvin, Jr., chairman of the board of Melvin Corporation and grandson of the founder, was visiting Paris next month, Arlington was keen to get the proposals as soon as possible. (Silmarax's consolidated balance sheets and income statements are shown in Exhibit A2.3.)

CASE STUDY 3: CLAVO

This case study presents some problems for you to identify. The date is December 1978. You are head of the Venezuelan territory of a New York bank. You have just received a visit from the president of a substantial Venezuelan manufacturer of fasteners (nuts, bolts, and so on) called CLAVO, seeking your bank's $5 million participation in a $15 million term loan to his company (the other lenders are American Express, which will lead the syndicate, and another unnamed U.S. bank). The term loan is to refinance short-term debt. At present you have $2 million outstanding on an offering basis to CLAVO, and CLAVO has been a regular borrower under a $2 million line of credit that expired recently.

CLAVO was created in 1958 by a small group of Venezuelan businessmen with an initial capital of Bs 500,000,[1] in order to provide an import saving local production. The company grew rapidly, and in 1978 its total revenues amounted to Bs 113 million (around $25 million). During its first 10 years of existence,the regional shareholding group was expanded to include a number of foreign partners from Argentina, Japan, and the United States that could

[1]Bs 4.4 = U.S.$1.00 as of Dec. 1978.

provide technical expertise and, in the case of Japan, guarantee a supply of raw materials. The company also built up a network of exclusive distributors to cover its home market, where it has a market share of 75%. The import of fasteners into Venezuela has been subject to very high tariffs and license controls since 1966 in order to protect local industry.

In the past five years, CLAVO has expanded rapidly. Sales in 1973 were Bs 32 million and are now nearly four times that figure. To meet its financing needs, CLAVO raised equity capital of Bs 22 million in 1977 on the local stock market and planned a bond issue of Bs 70 million in 1978, but this was deferred, as conditions in the bond market went against them.

Carlos Rodriguez, the president of the company, a strong manager who has been with CLAVO since it was founded, tells you that they will definitely raise Bs 50 million in a bond issue within the next two years to repay part of the term loan. Projections for the period of the term loan have been provided which show inter alia:

1. Costs of goods sold will improve from 58.9% to 56.9% of sales over seven years by the installation of cost controls and a computerized inventory control system.
2. Inventories will decline from the current level of 574 days to 491 days by 1982.
3. The company will modify its product mix to include a greater proportion of high-priced items whose market is growing rapidly and concentration on autos and the petroleum supply industry, since CLAVO is the only manufacturer in Venezuela which has met the quality standards set by the government for high-resistance fasteners.
4. Sales will grow as follows:

1979	19.6%	1980	13.5%	1981	11.1%	1982	10.4%
1983	10.2%	1984	9.4%	1985	9.3%		

In the past, you have felt CLAVO to be an important but difficult customer: important because of its strategic position in the Venezuelan economy, its rapid growth rate, and the influence of Rodriguez with the government (his sister is the wife of the minister of finance), but difficult because Rodriguez has led CLAVO into a big project involving participation in a steel mill to provide high-quality steel, which at present has to be imported, and this diverts funds from CLAVO. Further, although you have met with Rodriguez on many occasions, attempts to talk to financial officers in the company have proved disappointing. In the past, the company has also had difficulty "cleaning up" its line of credit.

The company is said to be profitable at present, with a big backlog of orders (six months). Although Venezuelan accounts are not totally reliable, its significant financial figures for the past five years are shown in Exhibit A3.1.

Exhibit A3.1 CLAVO Balance Sheet and Income Statements (year to October 31, millions of bolivars)

	1974	1975	1976	1977	1978
Cash	3	5	4	12	19
Receivables[1]	5	3	5	12	14
Inventories	40	66	76	86	120
Total Current Assets	48	74	85	110	153
Investments	1	1	2	2	6
Plant	25	33	40	53	62
Other Assets	7	9	13	43	49
TOTAL	81	117	140	208	270
Bank Debt	7	25	41	65	113
Long-Term Debt	—	2	6	4	4
Suppliers	17	19	16	34	37
Accrued Interest	1	1	1	1	2
Employee Profitsharing	2	4	5	5	6
Estimated Income Tax	3	5	5	5	4
Other Accruals	1	1	2	2	4
Dividends	1	1	1	1	1
Total Current Liabilities	32	58	77	117	171
Long-Term Debt	12	17	16	19	8
Due to Associates	3	3	2	11	7
Other Provisions	4	4	4	5	5
Minority Interests	1	1	2	2	3
Owner's Equity	29	34	39	54	76
	81	117	140	208	270
Sales	48	65	80	98	113
Net Income after Tax	6	8	8	10	5

[1]Net of discounted Receivables

Pricing on the proposed deal is attractive at 2% over LIBOR, and your territory is below budget on loan volume.

NOTES ON VENEZUELA

A recent study of Venezuela was generally very favorable and concluded as follows:

> Oil will remain of paramount importance to Venezuela in the next decade (export revenues from oil exceed $13 billion annually).
>
> The major policy concern is inflation. This is currently 12% in 1978, but it has been as low as 7.5% on average in 1975–1977.
>
> While external debt is generally considered large, "net debt" (allowing for international reserves) is relatively modest.
>
> Per capita gross national product is $3,500 per annum. Venezuela is a member of OPEC, and oil contributes 18% of gross national product.

QUESTIONS

1. Would you approve the term loan? If so, on what conditions? Suggest useful covenants.
2. If you do not approve the term loan, does that imply that you will try to get complete repayment—that is, cease offering basis loans? If so, what does that mean for your territory?

CASE STUDY 4: NORTHERN ENGINEERING INDUSTRIES LIMITED: A PROBLEM IN CASHFLOW ANALYSIS

This case study presents an exercise to be worked out by the reader: Northern Engineering Industries Limited is a substantial British company engaged in mechanical and combustion engineering. During 1978, it acquired some subsidiaries, principally Baldwin and Francis. The information reprinted here (Exhibit A4.1) is taken from the annual report published in April 1979. Find cash from operations using the transaction analysis form shown in Chapter 3 and sources and uses of cash.

The solution to this exercise is presented in Appendix 2.

Appendix 2 Solution to Northern Engineering Industries Problem

The following solution to the problem posed in Case Study 4 is suggested, but readers should note that it is based on certain assumptions explained in the notes to the transaction analysis. However, only two "plug" numbers are used, and both are quite small.

Sources of Cash (thousands of pounds)		Uses of Cash (thousands of pounds)	
Cash from Operations	19,432	Capital Expenditure	13,883
Sale of Investments	6,751	Acquisitions for Cash	6,299
Investment Income	2,444	Loan Stock Repaid	150
Dividends from Associates	502	Rationalization Costs	2,675
Assets Sold	742	Short-Term Debt Repaid	1,281
Net Decline in Cash	1,914	Payment to Minority Holders	730
		Dividends	5,254
		Advance Corporation Tax	1,369
		Tax on Exceptional Items	144
	31,785		31,785

NOTES TO THE TRANSACTION ANALYSIS SHEET

Begin with p. 10 of the annual report, then work through notes to financial statements.

Line 4. Tax expense is 6,717 of which 354 is attributed to associate companies (see note 3).

Line 6. Great care must be taken to deal separately with each extraordinary item to see its cash effect. Since rationalization costs are non-

Northern Engineering Industries Transaction Analysis Sheet

	Cash	Net Working Assets	Act Receivable	Fixed Assets	Subsidiaries and Investments	Goodwill	STD	Proposed Dividend	Loan Capital	Minority Interest	Preference Stock and Owner's Equity
1 31 Dec. 77	23,568	60,921	1,522	52,752	17,101	0	10,987	2,955	16,362	3,429	124,131
2 Trading Profit		+31,824									31,824
3 Interest		(6,363)									(1,360)
4 Tax					(354)						(6,717)
5 Minority Share										+984	(984)
6 Rationalization Cost	(2,675)										(2,675)
7 Surplus on Loan Stock	+97										+97
8 Profit on Investment	+6,751				(4,052)						+2,699
9 Tax on Exceptional Items	(144)										(144)
10 Divs. Proposed								+6,070			(6,070)
11 Divs. Paid	(5,254)							(5,254)			
12 Advance Corp. Tax	(1,369)		+1,369								
13 Associates Income		(1,258)			+1,258						
14 Depreciation		+7,271		(7,271)							
15 Investment Income	+2,444	(2,444)									
16 Dividends from Associates	+502				(502)						
17 Acquisitions	(6,299)	+6,371		+4,339	(2,516)	+1,947	+106			+2,836	+900
18 Paid to Minority Interest	(730)									(730)	
19 Loan Stock Repaid	(247)								(810)		563
20 Short-Term Debt Repaid	(1,281)						(1,281)				
21 Foreign Exchange Movements		(833)		(573)							(1,406)
22 Disposals	+742			(742)							
23 Capital Expenditure	(13,883)			+13,883							
24 Goodwill		(53)				+53					
25 Cash from Operations	+19,432	(19,432)									
31 Dec. 78	21,655	74,644	2,891	64,388	10,935	2,000	9,812	3,771	15,553	6,519	140,858

operating and nonrepeating, they are treated as a cash expense (see note 4).

Line 7. Although 97 is a gain, it represents a cash saving in payments to redeem loan stocks: Thus, loan stocks must have been redeemed below par value. This must be summarized with line 19 "Loan stock repaid or converted" (see note 4).

Line 8. Before dealing with profit on sale of unlisted investments entirely, we must establish original cost. This is found by subtracting 132 from 4,184 being the "other companies" line in note 10.

Line 9. From note 4 on p. 14.

Line 12. Advanced corporation tax is due on payment in cash of a dividend. Until it is offset against the company's current taxes it becomes a recoverable asset.

Line 13. From note 2 on p. 14. As we had already taken 31, 824 into net working assets, we must reverse out the 1,258 that is noncash income (accounting basis income).

Line 14. From note 2 on p. 14.

Line 15. All of the investment income is nonoperating income (note 2, p. 14), but 861 is a realized transaction gain and so is operating income.

Line 16. Dividends from associates from note 2 should be 551 not 502, but 502 will balance the column. Possibly some foreign exchange losses should be assigned to investments from net working assets, but then cash from operations would need adjustment. The missing figure is 49. Possibly a connection with the missing 53 in goodwill.

Line 17. This is difficult despite p. 12. The cash consideration of £6,299,000 is not the same as the amount in the directors' report (p. 8). Maybe cash balances were acquired. But if so, why 106 negative in the funds flow statement against "short-term deposits to cash"? Investments decrease by 2,723 as an investment becomes a subsidiary and is then consolidated. However, 207 appears to have been investments acquired in the transaction: hence, negative 2,516 to investments. Net working assets increases by 6,371 (6,890 + 3,518 − 2,570 + 640 + 130 − 2,237). And if goodwill goes up by 1,947, where is the remaining 53 to bring it to an end-year figure of 2,000? Is this related to the 106 negative—that is, an increase in short-term debt?

Line 19. From note 18, we know that loan capital decreased by 810, of which £417,569 was convertible loan stock. Other loans were repaid too in cash.

Line 21. From note 16, we know that 1,406 was charged against reserves of which 573 was for fixed assets (see note 8), so the balance must have been in net working assets, absent any foreign currency debt.

Line 22. In the absence of a reliable figure, we have to use the "plug" figure for disposals of fixed assets. This is 742. Any loss against book value might be hidden as a cost in capital expenditure. The figure of 1,210 for disposals (p. 12) is the net book value, not the cash received.

Line 24. See comments on line 17.

Appendix 3 Glossary of Financial Terms

ACCELERATE. (as in to accelerate a loan) To bring forward the date of repayment from some future date to the immediate present. This arises typically because of an Event of Default (see below). See also CROSS-ACCELERATION.

ACCEPTANCE. A type of Bill of Exchange. By accepting (or adding his acceptance to) a bill of exchange, the drawee undertakes to pay it on the maturity date. Accepted bills are often called acceptances. Acceptance can also be by endorsement. Bankers' acceptances are those where a bank has endorsed the bill and thus guarantees payment.

ACCEPTING HOUSE. Bank or financial organization whose specialty is adding its acceptance to its customer's bills so that they can be discounted in the discount market at favorable rates.

ACCOMMODATION PAPER. A note, trade acceptance, or draft endorsed by a person solely for the purpose of inducing a bank to lend money to a borrower when the latter's credit is not substantial enough to warrant a loan.

ACCOUNT PAYABLE. Money owed to creditors, usually suppliers.

ACCOUNT RECEIVABLE. Debtor. Money owed to the business.

ACCOUNTING PERIOD. Period of time from one balance sheet to the next. Period of the income statement, usually one year.

ACCOUNTING REPORTS. Balance sheet and income statement (profit and loss account).

ACCOUNTS RECEIVABLE FINANCING. Procedure whereby a specialized financial institution or bank makes loans against the pledge of accounts receivable.

ACCRUAL LIABILITY. Creditor, accounts payable, current liability. Accounting concept: income and expense for the accounting period must be included whether for cash or credit.

ACCUMULATED DEPRECIATION. Extent to which the fixed asset cost has been allocated to depreciate expense, since the asset was originally acquired. "Reserve" for depreciation. "Provision" for depreciation. Deducted from fixed assets.

ACCUMULATED PROFIT. Retained earnings. Balance of profit retained in the business. Increase in owner's equity due to profit earned but not paid out in dividends. Profit and loss account balance carried forward. Profit for more than one year.

ACQUISITION. The purchase of a company by another company

ADMINISTRATIVE EXPENSE. Cost of directing and controlling a business. Includes such expenses as director's fees, office salaries, office rent, lighting, heating, legal fees, auditor's fees, and accounting services, but not research, manufacturing, sales, or distribution expenses.

ADVANCE. A generic term for the ways in which a bank lends money, whether loan, overdraft, or discount.

ADVICE. Note telling a customer how much his or her account has been debited or credited for a transaction.

ADVISE A CREDIT. A letter of credit is opened when the importer's bankers mail it to their correspondent. It is advised when the correspondent passes it on to the exporter.

ADVISING BANK. The correspondent in the exporter's country that advises the credit.

AFFILIATE. A corporation or other organization related to another by being partly owned (not more than 50%). See also ASSOCIATE.

AMENDMENT. Alteration of the terms of a credit on the opener's instructions with the beneficiaries concerned.

AMORTIZATION. Depreciation, especially of intangible assets.

APPROPRIATION ACCOUNT. Statement of accumulated profit.

ARBITRAGE. Simultaneous purchase and sale of the same or equivalent items, to take advantage of a price discrepancy. The purchase of a security traded on two or more markets at the same time; also, occurs in the foreign exchange, commodity and money markets.

ARRANGEMENTS. Arrangements between correspondents about reimbursement for payments made on each other's behalf and about reciprocal business.

ASSET. Something owned that has a measurable cost. Fixed, current, or other assets. Includes claims on other persons.

ASSOCIATE. An associate is a partly owned company (less than 50% but more than 5%).

AT SIGHT. Payable on demand, like a check, as distinct from payable at a fixed period after acceptance.

AUTHORIZED CAPITAL. Amount of capital shareholders authorize a company to raise when a company starts business. Published in the memorandum and articles of association. Authorized capital can be increased after formation.

AUTHORIZED POSITIONS. The extent of the position in any currency that has been approved by management.

BAD DEBT. Debtor who fails to pay. Amount written off the expense.

BALANCE SHEET. A statement of the assets and liabilities of a company drawn up so as to give a fair view of the state of its affairs at a certain date.

BANKER'S ACCEPTANCE. See ACCEPTANCE.

BANKER'S PAYMENT. A payment instruction from one U.K. bank to another that is cleared like a check.

BC. Bill for collection. Most commonly the shipping documents will be released to the drawee against payment of a sight draft or acceptance of a time draft.

BENEFICIARY. Most commonly the exporter, the party who benefits from the credit by being able to negotiate documents for cash.

BILL COLLECTOR. The bank's representative who collects payment from drawees in exchange for bills of exchange drawn on them.

BILL OF EXCHANGE. A written instruction to a debtor to pay money on demand or in some cases at a determinable future data. A check is a type of bill of exchange. Defined in the U.K. under the Bills of Exchange Act 1882.

BILL OF LADING. A receipt given by a carrier to a shipper for goods received stating that the goods have been accepted for shipment and detailing the terms and conditions under which they will be transported. The original copy carries title to the goods, is negotiable, and is attached to the draft which is used to effect payment for shipment.

BILL PAYABLE. A bill of exchange which has to be paid; the opposite of a bill receivable.

BILLS DEPARTMENT. The department concerned with imports and exports. So called because it is common practice for an exporter to have a bill for the value of his goods collected from the importer by a bank in the importer's country.

BOND. Credit instrument that contains a promise to pay a specified amount of money at a fixed date or dates, usually more than 10 years after issuance, and a promise to pay interest periodically at stated dates.

BOOK VALUE. Two meanings: (1) value of assets in the books, or, (2) value of ordinary shares in the books.
(Computed: owner's equity less preference shares, divided by the number of ordinary shares.)

BORROWING LONG. Borrowing money for long periods.

BORROWING SHORT. Borrowing money for short periods, as distinct from borrowing long.

BULLET LOANS. These are term loans with repayment in full at the end of the period; there are no part payments along the way.

BUYING RATE. The rate at which the bank will buy foreign exchange from customers, paying them the equivalent in local currency.

CALL DEPOSITS. Deposits which are repayable on the demand either of the bank or of the depositor.

CAPITAL EQUIPMENT. Premises and plant, as distinct from current assets, such as stock.

CAPITAL RESERVE. Capital surplus. Capital profit. Not available for normal dividend. Not accumulated profit. Includes share premium. Not cash.

CAPITAL STOCK. Share capital in units of money.

CAPITAL SURPLUS. Capital reserve.

CAPITALIZATION. The summation of long-term debt, capital stock, and surplus. Also, "market capitalization" means total number of common shares multiplied by current share price.

CASH. Money assets of a business. Includes both cash in hand and cash at bank. Balance sheet current assets.

CASHFLOW. Cashflow normally means the cash resulting from sales minus operating expenses other than depreciation.

CASH DISCOUNT. Discount allowed to a debtor for early payment of a debt. Terms might be for payment within 10 days or net (not discount) for payment within one month.

CD. A certificate of deposit, usually negotiable by delivery, representing funds deposited at a bank.

CEILING. A limit imposed on something; for example, regulatory authorities may impose a ceiling on loans.

CHARGE. To take a charge is to take a mortgage or pledge over an asset.

CHARGE OFF. To reduce a loan by treating it as an accounting expense. Loans are charged off when considered uncollectible.

CIF. Cost, insurance, and freight, all of which are paid by the exporter and included in the invoice total. The main alternatives are C and F (cost and freight), where the importer looks after the insurance and is therefore not invoiced for it, and FOB (free on board), where the importer looks after both freight and insurance and is invoiced for neither.

CLEAN. Clean bills of lading bear no clauses. Shipping companies add clauses to bills of lading to protect themselves when cargo or packing appears defective.

CLEANUP. Describes the payment of all outstanding debts by a company to a bank. On occasion, a bank may require a cleanup (30–90 days) in order for the company to continue borrowing.

CLOSE. The legal process when the buyer's lawyer pays the purchase price to the seller's lawyer in exchange for the documents of title.

CLOSING. The procedure for signing a mortgage, or a syndicated loan or a bond issue. Also known as "signing."

CLOSING STOCK. Inventory at the end of the accounting period. Part of the computation of cost of goods sold.

COLLATERAL. Anything pledged or deposited in support of a loan over which the lender has taken a charge.

CO-MAKER. A person who signs a note in addition to the borrower to give extra security to the loan because of weakness of the borrower as an individual credit risk. A co-maker is distinguished in U.S. law from an endorser or guarantor in that, in a legal sense, the co-maker is jointly liable with the borrower for repayment. Whereas an endorser or guarantor is required to make good the loan only after certain legal technicalities have been fulfilled.

COMMERCIAL PAPER. Consists of promissory notes of large business concerns of high credit standing, usually maturing in 30, 60, or 90 days, which are bought and sold in the open market.

COMMITMENT. Any extension of credit to which the bank is committed, whether advance, letter of credit, guarantee, loan or overdraft.

COMMON STOCK. Ordinary shares.

CONFIRM A CREDIT. A bank which opens a credit is liable under it; a bank which advises a credit is not liable under that credit unless it confirms it, thereby guaranteeing payment whether the opening bank pays or not.

CONFIRMATION COMMISSION. A bank's charge for confirming a credit.

CONTINGENT LIABILITY. A liability not generally recorded on the balance sheet. May or may not become an actual liability. Liabilities to make payments if certain things happen—for example, if an exporter presents documents under a credit. Different from direct liabilities, such as liabilities to repay debts. A guarantee is often a contingent liability.

CONTRA. A vital term of double-entry bookkeeping. Books are a record of transactions between debtors and creditors; every entry to the credit of a creditor's account for money or value owed to the creditor must be matched by equal and opposite contra entries to the debit of the debtor's account for money or value owed by the debtor.

CONVENTION. Assumption made in accounting. Many accounting concepts arise from assumptions that have proven to be practicable.

CONVERTIBLE BONDS. Bonds issued by a corporation which may be converted by the holder into stock of the corporation within a specified time period and a specified price.

CORPORATE RESOLUTION. A document given to a bank by a corporation defining the authority vested in each of its officers who may sign for and otherwise conduct the business of the corporation with the bank. These powers are granted by the Board of Directors of the firm.

CORRESPONDENT. A bank in another place which performs services, particularly making and receiving payments to the debit or credit of a nostro account in their books.

COUNTERPARTY. The party with whom a bank makes a contract covering its contract with a customer, when it squares its position.

COVENANT. A promise made by a borrower in a term loan agreement.

COVER. When a bank instructs its correspondent to pay out more than it has in its account, it has to put the account in funds again (or cover) by instructing another bank to pay the correspondent. A very important part of foreign exchange activity.

COVERED FORWARD. A Trader, who is to receive foreign currency and will want to exchange it for his own, covers himself forward against the risk of loss in exchange by selling the foreign currency immediately to his bankers, so that he knows how much of his own currency they will receive, whatever happens to the exchange rates since he fixes the future rate at the time of the deal. See also FORWARD CONTRACTS.

CREDIT LIMIT/CREDIT LINES. The limits up to which a bank is prepared to lend money or grant credit to a customer. A line of credit is not normally a legal commitment, only a willingness to do business.

CREDIT TRANSACTION. Transaction that incurs (accrues) liability. No cash is paid or received until later.

CREDITOR. Payable, account payable, liability. Money owed to other parties. Current or long-term liability.

CREDITOR'S CLAIMS. Liabilities.

CROSS ACCELERATION. The process of making a term credit immediately payable because another term credit has become capable of being made immediately payable.

CROSS DEFAULT. The right to call an Event of Default under a loan agreement when another lender in another agreement has called an Event of Default. This right is frustrated if the other lender grants a waiver.

CURRENT ACCOUNT. The most common form of bank account, against which one can write checks. Commercial current accounts—between companies or between companies and their directors, for instance, are accounts that may be settled on demand, as distinct from loan accounts that are not settled before due.

CURRENT ASSETS. Assets which are normally realized in cash or used up in operations during one operating period (normally one year). Includes cash, debtors, inventory, and prepaid expenses.

CURRENT LIABILITY. Liability due for payment within one operating cycle (usually but not always one year).

CURRENT RATIO. Ratio of current assets to current liabilities. Measure of liquidity.

D/A. Documents against acceptance, as distinct from D/P, when the documents are released only against payment.

DEBENTURE. An obligation, a bond. Long-term debt. May be secured or unsecured.

DEBT SERVICE COVERAGE RATIO. See interest coverage ratio. Sometimes also includes required payments with interest payments (see Chapter 6).

DEFERRED INCOME. Income received in advance of being earned and recognized. Normally left as a current liability on the balance sheet until the sale is made and the income recognized.

DEFERRED SHARES. Shares of a company, ranking for dividend after preference or preferred and ordinary shares.

DEFERRED STOCK. Deferred shares.

DEMURRAGE. Charges incurred as a result of delay in clearing goods at a port.

DEPRECIATION. The amount by which the assets of a business are judged to have diminished during the year. Tax authorities limit the amount of depreciation which may be allowed to diminish a company's profits. Allocation of the cost of a fixed asset to expense over its working life. Measure of the cost of using the fixed asset.

DEPRECIATION EXPENSE. Depreciation (at cost) during the accounting period. Not the same as accumulated depreciation except in the first year of the fixed asset.

DIRECTORS' LOANS. In small companies, the directors are often the main shareholders. They cannot withdraw their capital from the company without complicated legal procedure, and therefore they often finance its growth by loans rather than capital.

DOCUMENTARY CREDIT LINE. The maximum value of documentary credits which a bank will have outstanding for a customer at one time.

DOCUMENTARY CREDITS. Documentary credits are banker's promises to pay for specified shipping documents covering shipments on certain items.

DRAFT. Bill of exchange. Often used in banks in a restricted sense to mean bills or checks drawn by a bank on its branch or correspondent.

ENDORSE. To sign one's name, and usually on the back of a check or draft.

ENDORSED IN BLANK. Cargo is delivered in accordance with the orders endorsed on the bill of lading. If it is endorsed in blank, the cargo may be delivered in acccordance with the collecting bank's order.

ENDORSEMENT. A person transfers his right to receive an amount of money. The endorser accepts the liability of making payment on the instrument of the original maker if prior endorsers fail to do so.

ENDOWMENT POLICY. A type of life insurance policy under which the insurance company promises to pay on a certain date or at death, whichever is earlier.

ENTITY. Accounting concept: accounting reports are prepared for a specific entity.

ENTRIES. Transactions in a bank are entered in the books. Hence, transactions passing through the books are described as book entries or simply, entries. You pass entries when you make out vouchers; you post entries when you enter them in a ledger.

EQUIPMENT. Fixed asset if acquired for long-term use and not for resale. Recorded in the balance sheet at cost less depreciation, not at market value.

EQUITY. The shareholders' stake in a business.

EURODOLLARS. Dollars owned by nonresidents of the United States and held in bank accounts outside the United States.

EVENT OF DEFAULT. A covenant, term or a condition of a long term loan which when broken by the borrower causes the loan to become immediately due and payable. See also ACCELERATE.

EXCESS. The amount by which an overdraft or other credit exceeds its authorized limits.

EXCHANGE CONTRACT. Contract between a bank and a company to exchange one currency for another, generally either at a fixed future date or spot (for example, two business days after the deal is made).

EXCHANGE POSITION. A bank's spot or forward assets or liabilities in foreign currency.

EXPIRY DATES. Letters of credit have two expiry dates—the last date for shipment and the last date for negotiation of the documents.

FACE VALUE. Nominal value of shares. Not the book (owner's equity) value or market value.

FACTORING. Procedure whereby a specialized finance company or bank purchases the accounts receivable of a firm without recourse.

FEDERAL FUNDS. Sight claims on Federal Reserve banks or the U.S. Treasury. A method whereby member banks may adjust their reserve balance with the Federal Reserve bank. Generally borrowed for one day.

FIDUCIARY. An individual, corporation, or association, such as a bank or trust company, to whom certain assets are given to hold in trust, according to a trust agreement.

FIRST PRESENTATION. The drawee of a sight bill (that is, a bill of exchange payable at once) is expected to require a day or two to arrange funds to pay it, and payment of first presentation is unusual. A usance bill, on the other hand, must be paid on the due date. By deferring acceptance, a drawee defers eventual payment.

FISCAL STATEMENT. A statement for a yearly period at the end of which a firm determines its financial condition without regard to the calendar year.

FIXED ASSETS. Such assets as land, plant, and equipment acquired for long-term use in the business and not for resale. Charged to overhead expense periodically as depreciation. Recorded in the balance sheet at cost less depreciation, not market value. Sometimes revalued periodically if accounting principles permit (GAAP does not).

FIXED EXPENSES. Fixed expenses occur whatever volume is produced. Compare variable expenses.

FLOATING CHARGE. Charge over a debtor's fluctuating assets, such as the inventory which the debtor undertakes to convert into a charge for a fixed amount if the creditor demands that the debtor do so.

FOB. Free on board. The importer arranges and pays for freight and insurance and is therefore invoiced for neither. See also CIF.

FORWARD CONTRACTS. You may buy or sell a currency for future delivery fixing the future exchange rate today. This is a forward contract. Forward rates reflect the cost of interest on the money to be used.

GOODWILL. Value of the name, reputation, or intangible assets of the business. In accounting, this is only recorded when the business is purchased, and it is wholly amortized. Represents the excess of price paid over the value of the net assets acquired.

GROSS PROFIT. Difference between sales and cost of goods sold. Profit computed before charging for selling and administrative expenses, and other expenses.

GROSS PROFIT PERCENTAGE. Measure of profitability computed as:

$$\frac{\text{Gross profit}}{\text{Net sales}} \times 100\%$$

INCOME. Earnings, profit, revenue. Sometimes used to mean sales and all forms of income benefits, not necessarily in cash.

INDEMNITY. Generally, a form letter in which a bank undertakes to do something and to refund any cost or loss the beneficiary may suffer from some specified event.

INFLATION ACCOUNTING. A set of rules which attempts to adjust historic cost accounts to allow for the changes in values arising from rates of inflation. Assumes that accounting should record "value."

INTANGIBLE ASSET. Asset which cannot actually be touched, for example copyrights and goodwill.

INTERBANK MARKET. Where banks deal extensively with each other, covering their positions in local currency and foreign exchange.

INTEREST COVERAGE RATIO. Earnings before interest and taxes divided by interest expense.

INVENTORY. Stock of goods on hand for resale. It includes stores and supplies, and is valued at the lower of cost or market value, not selling price.

It is increased by purchases and decreased by cost of goods sold. Also, a balance sheet current asset.

IRREVOCABLE CREDIT. Bankers' promise to pay in exchange for shipping documents covering shipment on certain terms that can not be revoked by the bank that opens it (issues it) without the permission of the beneficiary.

ISSUED CAPITAL. Share capital actually issued by a company. See also AUTHORIZED CAPITAL. Price at which a share is first sold by a company; normally the nominal value plus share premium or less share discount. May be ordinary, preference or deferred shares, not bonds or debentures.

LETTER OF CREDIT. Bankers' promise to pay in exchange for shipping documents covering shipment on certain terms.

LIMITED COMPANY. Company whose shareholders have limited their liability to the amounts that they subscribe to the shares which they hold.

LINE OF CREDIT. An indication of willingness by a lender to do business by way of extending credit to the borrower up to the figure specified. Not a commitment to lend. Normally reviewed annually but subject to cancellation without notice.

LIQUID. The liquid assets of a company are those which can easily be realized, such as cash and marketable securities.

LONG. A position in which assets exceed liabilities; for example, a bank whose contracts to buy dollars for sterling exceed its contract to sell dollars for sterling is long in dollars and short in sterling. Also called "overbought."

LONG-TERM LIABILITY. Liability not due for payment within one year. Bonds, debentures, or loans. Holders are creditors and receive interest; they are not shareholders.

MANAGEMENT CONTROL RETURNS. A class of accounting returns whose object is to enable management to control the business more effectively.

MARGIN COLLATERAL. A bank lends only a proportion of the quoted value of any security, in case the market value diminishes. The margin is the difference between the value of the collateral and the amount lent.

MARGIN (PROFIT). The element of profit in sales after deducting sales costs, usually measured as a percentage of sales.

MARKETABLE STOCK. Shares and bonds which are traded on stock exchanges and are correspondingly easy to market. Because of marketing difficulties, banks are usually not keen on unquoted stocks or bonds as collateral.

MATERIALS. Directors' valuation of these in a balance sheet is generally at cost or present market value, whichever is lower. The trading profit is affected by this valuation.

MATURITY. The date on which a loan or deposit is due to be repaid.

MEMORANDUM AND ARTICLES OF ASSOCIATION. The documents setting out a company constitution.

MONEY MARKET. The market in which banks, finance houses, and major companies lend each other their surplus funds.

MORTGAGE. Long-term loan normally secured on a fixed asset. Long-term liability.

NET CURRENT ASSETS. The amount by which a company's current assets exceed its current liabilities.

NET WORTH. The amount which would be divided among the shareholders if a company were to liquidate. It is the sum of the paid-up capital and all the reserves. Tangible net worth is the amount less any intangible assets.

NOMINAL VALUE. Face value of shares. Authorized and issued share capital in the balance sheet shows the nominal value of the shares separately from any premium or discount. Not the book value or market value of shares.

NOSTRO ACCOUNT. An account belonging to our bank at another bank (that is, our own operating account). See also VOSTRO ACCOUNT.

ON DEMAND. The paying bank will pay as soon as the draft is presented to it by another bank or reaches it by mail.

OPEN A CREDIT. A credit is opened when the importer's bank issues it, as distinct from being advised by the bank in the exporter's country. The importer is sometimes referred to as the opener of the credit, though this is not correct.

OPENING STOCK. Inventory at the beginning of the accounting period.

ORDINARY SHARES. Share capital. Part of owner's equity in the balance sheet. Holders are entitled to dividends recommended by the directors. Net preference shares. Possible values: face or nominal value, market value, issue price (including any premium), book value (total owner's equity less the nominal value of preference shares).

OVERDRAFT LIMIT. Customers may draw up to a certain limit more than they have in their accounts, and interest is charged on the actual day-to-day debit balance in the account that results.

OVERHEADS. The administrative expenses of a business, often fixed costs, such as rent.

OWNER'S EQUITY. Net worth. Amount due to owners of the business. Increased by profits. Reduced by losses, and dividends. Assets minus liabilities equals owner's equity.

P&L. Profit and loss account. Also income statement.

PATENT. Legal right to exploit an invention. Asset in the balance sheet. Recorded at cost less depreciation under the heading "Other Assets."

PLANT. Manufacturing equipment and machinery. Fixed asset if acquired for use and not for resale. Often used to describe both a factory and the equipment in it.

PLOUGH BACK PROFIT. Retain net profit in the business by carrying it forward in the profit and loss account instead of distributing it in dividends.

PORTFOLIO. A group term for assets, including securities, acceptances, discounts, loans, and overdrafts. One also talks in a more detailed sense of a portfolio of acceptances.

POST. Enter transactions in the bank's books, either by hand or by machine.

PREFERRED STOCK. Also known in some countries as preference share.

PREFERENCE SHARE. Share which entitles the holder to fixed dividends (only) in preference to the dividends for ordinary shares. On liquidation, normally entitled only to the nominal value. No right to share in profits, except where specified.

PREMIUM. Sum paid periodically to an insurance company for insuring one's life or property. In the case of forward currency, the amount which it costs more than spot currency. For instance, if spot U.S. $ dollars cost 2.3950 per British pound and the one-month premium is 12 points, you get only $2.3938 in exchange for £1 if you fix a contract for delivery one month ahead.

PREPAYMENTS. Items, such as rent, which have to be paid in advance.

PRICE/EARNINGS RATIO. The ratio between the price to be paid for a company and its net earnings or profit. Multiply the number of shares issued by the official quoted price, and compare this figure with the last published net profit.

PROFIT AND LOSS ACCCOUNT. The account in which companies record the amount of profit they retain or the amount of loss they have not yet recovered. Income statement. Statement showing sales, costs, expenses, and profit for an acccounting period.

PROVISION. Strictly means liability, but often has several different meanings: reserve (for example, future income tax liability), accumulation, (accumulated depreciation), expense (for example, depreciation expense), accrual (for example, accrued expense, liability).

PUBLISHED FINANCIAL STATEMENTS. Balance sheet, profit and loss account, and statement of accumulated profit, with comparative figures and notes disclosing information.

RECOGNITION OF PROFIT. As accounting concept: Profit is not recognized and recorded until realized (in cash or accounts receivable). By contrast, losses are often recognized when goods are shipped to the customer, not when the order is received or when the customer pays for the goods.

RECONCILIATION. Proving an account is right by comparing it in detail with a statement of the same account in someone else's books.

REDEEMABLE PREFERENCE SHARES. Preference shares which may be repurchased by the company from the shareholders. Part of owner's equity. Not ordinary shares.

RESERVE. Strictly means accumulated profit. Used more vaguely. See REVENUE RESERVE, PROVISION.

RETIRE. Collections of shipping documents are retired by being paid for and released. Debt is retired by being paid.

RETAINED EARNINGS. Accumulated profits, available for dividend. Part of owner's equity.

REVALUATION. Sometimes fixed assets are revalued from historic cost to current values. The difference is credited to reserves.

REVENUE. Earnings, income, profit; sometimes also used to mean sales.

REVENUE RESERVE. Profit available for dividends. Accumulated profit and general reserve. Retained earnings.

SCHEDULES. Collection schedules give details of the documents being handled and instructions on how to handle them. Accounting schedules, on the other hand, usually give tabulated information about particular aspects of the business.

SECURED LOAN. A loan against security in which the lender can realize an asset if the borrower fails to pay, as opposed to an unsecured loan which gives the lender no claim over any asset.

SECURITIES. Documents of title to investments, such as share certificates and bonds.

SECURITY. Collateral such as property (real or personal), goods, or documents of title.

SHARE. Document certifying ownership of shares in a company.

SHARE PREMIUM. Excess of original sales price of a share over its face or nominal value. Not available for dividend.

SHORT. A position in which liabilities exceed assets. For example, if contracts to sell marks for sterling exceed contracts to buy, one is short in marks and long in sterling. Also called "oversold."

SIGHT CREDITS. Letters of credit calling for sight drafts, as distinct from usance credits calling for usance drafts.

SIGHT DRAFTS. Drafts payable on demand (at sight), as distinct from usance drafts payable a certain period after acceptance or date.

SPOT. For payment two business days ahead: this gives everyone time to handle all the paperwork conveniently. The normal term for dealings in the foreign exchange market.

SQUARE. A position in which asset and liabilities are matched. One sometimes talks of a square position if it is matched overall, even if it is oversold one month and overbought six. Also called "matched."

STOCK. Inventory. Supply of finished goods, raw material, or both. Valued at the lower of manufacturing cost or market value.

STOCKHOLDER. Shareholder.

STRAIGHT-LINE DEPRECIATION. Depreciation method charging off the cost of a fixed asset equally over the years of its working life. See also DEPRECIATION.

SUBORDINATION. An agreement between a company and some of its creditors not to repay them before it repays the bank.

SUM OF THE YEAR'S DIGITS. This is a method of depreciation with emphasis on early years. If the life of an asset is five years, depreciation in the first year will be 5/15 (15 being the sum of 5 + 4 + 3 + 2 + 1), hence the name. In the second year it will be 4/15 and so on.

TANGIBLE ASSET. Asset that can be physically identified or touched. Sometimes means only those assets that have a definite value—that is, excludes intangible assets, goodwill, and research and development expenditures or other expenditures that have been capitalized.

TANGIBLE NET WORTH. This is the sum of all reserves and capital funds less any intangible assets. It is "true" owners' equity, as far as that can be determined.

TIME DEPOSITS. Deposits placed with the bank for a fixed period, as distinct from call deposits. Interest is normally payable at maturity.

TERM LOANS. Loans made by the bank for a fixed period, as distinct from demand loans and from overdrafts, which fluctuate in amount. The time for interest payment varies from loan to loan.

TRADE CREDITORS AND TRADE DEBTORS. Many manufacturers have to allow their customers time to pay for goods purchased and correspondingly demand credit from their own suppliers, without which they are unable to buy from them. You owe to a trade creditor; a trade debtor owes to you.

TRADE INVESTMENT. Investment in shares or debentures of another company in the same trade or industry. Long-term investment. "Other asset" in the balance sheet. Valued at cost, unless there is a substantial loss.

TRADING PROFIT. The difference between the value of sales and the total cost of goods sold. Carried into profit and loss account.

TRANSACTION. Change in two items in the balance sheet. Cash or credit transaction. May be sale, purchase, cash receipt, cash payment, or accounting adjustment.

TRANSFER DEED. An instruction signed by both the seller and the buyer of shares and bonds, or their agents, to the registrar of a company to transfer the shares or bonds into the buyer's name.

TRUE AND FAIR. Accounting concept. Balance sheet and income statement show a "true and fair view" of the business, in accordance with generally accepted accounting principles.

TRUST RECEIPT. Receipt given by a customer to a bank for documents released to him before payment of the bill. He holds the goods in trust for the bank to whom he undertakes to pay the sale proceeds, to meet the bill in due course. Not normally a legal claim, it may help a bank establish a legal right over the goods against another party with a claim.

TURNOVER. Total sales.

UNCERTAINTY. Limitation of accounting. Uncertainty at the end of each accounting period makes it difficult to determine the "true and fair" position. Uncertainty arises from incomplete transactions, market value of inventory, working life of fixed assets for depreciation calculations, realizable values of current assets, and contingent liabilities not yet known or calculable.

UNREALIZED. Profit is realized only when it is actually received—in the case of exchange position, when the forward contracts have matured.

UNWIND. Square the position by buying to cover an oversold position or selling to cover an overbought position.

USANCE CREDIT. Letter of credit calling for bills maturing at a determinable future date, as distinct from a sight credit calling for bills payable at sight.

USANCE DRAFT. A draft payable on a specified date.

VALUE. Several meanings:

1. Accounting value—value according to accounting concepts, appropriate to the particular asset. Fixed assets valued at cost less depreciation. Current assets generally valued at cost or lower realizable value.
2. Market value—realizable value of inventory in the normal course of business (not in liquidation).
3. Real value—not known in accounting.

VARIABLE EXPENSES. Expenses that vary with the volume produced, as distinct from fixed expenses, which do not.

VOSTRO ACCOUNT. An account at our bank belonging to another bank.

VOUCHERS. Each book entry in a bank arises from a voucher—that is, either a check or deposit slip prepared by a customer, or a slip prepared by bank staff on customer's instructions.

WAIVER. An agreement by a lender to forgive a broken condition or covenant in a term loan (usually for a short period) which would otherwise give rise to an Event of Default.

WASTE. An old banking term which in accounting language would be a journal. A large sheet on which the waste clerk analyzes and adds up all the different types of bank book entries during the day. The various totals balance with corresponding totals in the other parts of the bank, which proves the accuracy of the entries. That is, for every credit, there must be a corresponding debit.

WORKING CAPITAL. Current assets less current liabilities.

WORKING CAPITAL RATIO. Ratio of current assets to current liabilities. Indicates the liquidity of the business.

WOUND UP. A company is dissolved by being wound up with the court's permission.

WRITE DOWN. To decrease; an asset when it is written down is decreased in its recorded value.

WRITE OFF. When a loan is written off, it is reduced to zero on the books of the lender. See also CHARGE OFF.

Index

Breinigsville, PA USA
09 September 2010
245085BV00006B/9/P